Xmas 19

To our
Special

Sandy, Jim, Sandal

DANCERS
TO REMEMBER
The photographic art of
GORDON ANTHONY

DANCERS
TO REMEMBER
The photographic art of
GORDON ANTHONY

FOREWORD BY DAME MARGOT FONTEYN

RIZZOLI
NEW YORK

Dedication

To Arnold Haskell in friendship and gratitude for his help and co-operation at the beginning of my 'Balletic' photographic career and his continued friendship and patronage afterwards.

Published in the United States of America by:
Rizzoli International Publications, Inc.
712 Fifth Avenue, New York, N.Y. 10019

LC 80-59494
ISBN 0 8478 0271 X

Printed and bound in Great Britain

Acknowledgments

Many thanks are due to Alexander Shuvalov, Curator of the Theatre Museum for permission to publish my photographs, which are now in their possession, and for the unstinting help of his staff, especially Katherine Haile, Antony Lathan and Sarah Woodcock. Also to Peter Williams for his encouragement and advice and Mary Clarke for much help and for commissioning the articles from which this book was born. To Kathleen Gordon CBE and Penelope Spencer for their hard work in checking the proofs owing to my bad eyesight. To Brian Upcott for making excellent reproductions from my old books, to Felix Fonteyn for some superb copying and printing from old photographs and to John Travis, Archivist of London Festival Ballet, for help with Appendix 1.

GORDON ANTHONY 1980

Foreword

2

Gordon Anthony is one of the great photographers whose work gains with the perspective of time and, like Hoppé, de Meyer and Beaton, his pictures of dancers have a very personal stamp that is instantly recognizable.

All his life he has had an intense enthusiasm for the theatre and, in particular, for ballet which he understands from the point of view of expression in movement. When he launched out into ballet photography what attracted him was not the art of photography but its use to depict the elusive and crucial moments of dance. In fact he had little knowledge of conventional camera techniques but, like a painter obsessed with the idea of portraying movement as he observes it, Anthony developed his own techniques as necessity dictated. The individuality of his work was achieved by knowing before each sitting exactly which movements he wanted to catch in order to sum up the entire characterization of a role, and in preparing a background composition that would re-create the atmosphere of the ballet portrayed. There is an example in the photograph of myself in *Façade*, taken in front of a zany cow which he drew himself. It conjures up perfectly the jaunty mood of the ballet. More often he used simple projections of shadows to suggest the decor and, on occasion, produced strikingly dramatic results with shadow-play figures of related characters. I like the simplicity and clarity of all his photographs – everything that needs to be said is there without clutter.

As a record of dance at a particular period his pictures are without comparison. The lithographs and prints of mid-nineteenth-century ballet pay little attention to male dancers, and the early photographs are similarly biased – they show a series of ballerinas in one costume or another gazing enigmatically at the camera. Not until the beginning of this century was there more than a very occasional attempt to show something of the spirit and style of the choreography and even then it was difficult to avoid the 'posed' effect. Gordon Anthony produced work that combines action with atmosphere and has the high standard, photographically, of 'still' pictures.

Quite early in his career he had the opportunity to become a regular contributer to the 'glossies' – the *Bystander* and *Sketch* – which usually featured a full-page theatrical photograph every fortnight. This of course gave him a passport to the world of theatre and ballet and he photographed almost every important artist who came to London during the interesting post-Diaghilev Ballets Russes years. His work for the magazines and his books on dancers probably did more than is realized to popularize dancing, and especially British ballet which was then struggling against a certain amount of disbelief that any but foreigners could become stars.

It is very right that Gordon Anthony's valuable collection of negatives should now form part of The Theatre Museum London archives, and I am extremely happy that this book will make many of the pictures available to enthusiasts of both photography and dance. They are instructive, amusing, quaint and very nostalgic – a record to be treasured.

DAME MARGOT FONTEYN DE ARIAS

Youly Algaroff   An athletically graceful yet virile classical danseur noble, roles such as Albrecht in *Giselle* suited him perfectly. He was born of Russian parents in Simferopol and studied under Eugenia Edouardova (ex Maryinsky) in Berlin, and with Boris Kniaseff in Paris and toured with Yvette Chauviré. In 1945 Algaroff joined Roland Petit's Ballets des Champs-Elysées as soloist. In 1946 he joined the Nouveau Ballet de Monte Carlo. 1953 found him as an étoile of the Paris Opera Ballet and 1960 partnering Chauviré, their ballerina assoluta, in a Russian tour.

In 1965 Youly Algaroff became an impresario in Paris.

Algeranoff   Character dancer, choreographer, and ballet master, whose real name was Algernon Harcourt Essex. He was born in London in 1903 and died in Australia in 1967. Algeranoff made his debut with Pavlova's company in 1921 and stayed with her for ten years; after that he worked with the Markova Dolin Ballet. Also the International Ballet, and the Borovansky Ballet in Australia for both of which he was a soloist and teacher, and occasionally as a choreographer.

For the de Basil Ballets Russes, Algeranoff was a soloist and character dancer; with them he created the role of the Astrologer in *Le Coq d'Or*, the type of role he specialized in. He settled in Australia and opened his own studio where he taught character and oriental dancing as well as classical ballet. He wrote a book on his life with Pavlova's company, *My Years with Pavlova* (1957).

Alicia Alonso Considered a dancer of great brilliance and dramatic ability. Born in Havana, Cuba in 1917 and trained by Fedorova and Anatole Vilzak, she started her career in musicals, joining the Ballet Caravan in 1939 and American Ballet Theatre in 1941, creating the highly dramatic role of Lizzie in Agnes de Mille's *Fall River Legend* for them at the Metropolitan Opera House, New York in 1948. She was prima ballerina with the company during their season at Covent Garden in 1946.

Decorated by the Cuban Government in 1947, Alicia Alonso formed the Alicia Alonso Ballet – which became the Ballet de Cuba in 1955 – of which she was the ballerina assoluta. She danced twice in Russia and produced *Giselle* for the Paris Opera Ballet with herself in the title role in 1952.

Antonio (Ruiz Soler) Born in Seville in 1921, he studied with Realitol. With his cousin Rosario he made his debut at Liège at the age of seven – a childhood partnership which lasted on and off for over twenty years. They travelled all over the world and made their London debut in 1951.

Antonio had two other partners, Rosita Segovia and Carmen Rojas, and formed a Spanish Ballet Company with them which I saw in London, but somehow Spanish dancing lends itself grudgingly to ballet as such.

Antonio himself may be described as dynamic. He became famous for his dancing of the Zapateado. He was considered one of Spain's greatest virtuoso dancers.

Pearl Argyle Born in Johannesburg, South Africa, as Pearl Wellman in 1910, she came to England in 1926, making her debut as a student with Marie Rambert at the Ballet Club, eventually becoming her ballerina and creating for her the leading role in de Valois's *Bar aux Folies Bergères* and the Mermaid for Andrée Howard. For Ashton she created leading roles in *Mars and Venus, Les Masques, Valentine's Eve*, and for Antony Tudor Hebe in *The Descent of Hebe*. Furthermore, she danced for Les Ballets 1933 and the Camargo Society before finally joining the Vic-Wells Ballet for a short period after Markova left in 1935. Amongst the roles she created for the company were the Princess in de Valois's *Le Roi Nu*, and the fairy in Ashton's *Baiser de la Fée*, in which latter ballet she excelled both as dancer and actress.

Pearl Argyle was noted as much for her great beauty, charm, and 'star' qualities, as she was for her dancing abilities. She left England in 1938 for America, where she appeared in several films until her tragically sudden death of a heart attack in 1947.

Frederick Ashton The first English choreographer of note and considered one of the greatest in the world today – his work appears to be a cross between that of Bournonville and Petipa.

Ashton was born in Ecuador of English parents and started life in business but decided to become a dancer and joined Marie Rambert's school in 1926. He left for a year to dance with Ida Rubenstein's company where he studied with Massine and Nijinska, then returned to Marie Rambert where he began his career under her tuition and guidance.

Ashton's first ballet, created in 1926, was *A Tragedy of Fashion* – with himself and Marie Rambert in the leading roles. After dancing and choreographing many ballets for her he 'flew the nest' to join the Vic-Wells Ballet where his work developed further.

Ashton has choreographed ballets for musicals, films and for major companies all over the world, but his most popular work was done for the Royal Ballet, *Apparitions, Baiser de la Fée, Ondine, Daphnis and Chloë, Sylvia, La Fille Mal Gardée, Symphonic Variations, Marguerite and Armand*, to mention but a few. He became director of the Royal Ballet after de Valois retired in 1963 and he was, in 1970, given the title of Founder Choreographer of the Royal Ballet.

Ashton was awarded the CBE, and the Danish Order of Dannebrog; he received a knighthood in 1962 and was made a Companion of Honour in 1970.

Sir Frederick Ashton is still working and created a special ballet for the sixtieth birthday of Dame Margot Fonteyn which was given at Covent Garden on 23 May 1979.

Irina Baronova Ballerina and film star. Born in Petrograd 1919, Baronova trained under Preobrajenska in Paris, making her debut at the Paris Mogador in 1930. In 1932 Balanchine 'discovered' her with Riabouchinska and Toumanova – famous in the thirties as the Baby Ballerinas – when he engaged them for the Ballets Russes in Monte Carlo.

At the age of fourteen Baronova was dancing ballerina roles and creating modern ones. She appeared with the Russian ballet at the Alhambra and at Covent Garden, during which period she created leading roles in *Les Cent Baisers, Choreartium, Les Présages, Le Beau Danube*, and *Le Coq d'Or*.

In classical ballets Baronova danced *Lac des Cygnes, The Firebird*, and *Petrouchka*.

In 1939 Baronova left to dance for American companies and in films. Now retired, Baronova still teaches occasionally.

Svetlana Beriosova A classical ballerina of surpassing grace, charm and elegance. Beriosova was born in Kaunas of Lithuanian parents, her father being Nicholas Beriosoff, a former character dancer who taught her himself. She made her debut with the Ballet Russe de Monte Carlo in 1941. She then joined several companies in succession – the Ottawa Ballet Company, the de Cuevas Ballet and the Metropolitan Ballet Company as ballerina until she joined the Sadler's Wells Theatre Ballet in 1950. Eventually became one of the leading ballerinas of the Royal Ballet at Covent Garden, dancing in all their classical ballets and creating other modern leading roles in *Rinaldo and Armida*, *Baiser de la Fée*, *Enigma Variations*, *Antigone* and *Perséphone*. In the last ballet she recited in French with a voice whose great beauty and depth equalled that of her dancing.

Despite all her roles Beriosova still found time to be a guest artist in Australia and at famous opera houses on the Continent. She retired from dancing in 1975, and now coaches dancers in her great roles.

David Blair   English principal dancer, producer and teacher. He was born in Halifax in 1932, had his early training with the Royal Academy of Dancing and won a scholarship into the Sadler's Wells School in 1946, from which he graduated into the Sadler's Wells Theatre Ballet a year later as soloist.

In 1951 David Blair created his first leading role in John Cranko's *Harlequin in April*, followed by Captain Belaye in *Pineapple Poll* in the same year.

By 1955 Blair had become a principal dancer for the Sadler's Wells Ballet at Covent Garden dancing leading roles in both classical and modern ballets. He created roles in *The Prince of the Pagodas*, *Antigone*, *Elektra*, *Romeo and Juliet* and above all Colas in *La Fille Mal Gardée*, which was considered his best.

Blair appeared as a guest artist at La Scala, partnering Margot Fonteyn, and reproduced many of the classic ballets abroad. He was awarded the CBE in 1964 and retired from the Royal Ballet in 1968. In 1970 he returned as a teacher and occasional guest artist. He died in London in 1976.

Patricia Bowman A lovely blonde American ballerina who was born in Washington D.C. and studied ballet with Fokine, Legat and Egorova.

Patricia Bowman was principal dancer for Massine at the Roxy in New York and for the Mordkin Ballet Company. She joined Ballet Theatre in 1940, but most of her work was in American musicals and with the Chicago Opera Company. She retired to teach in New York.

Edouard Borovansky Czech character dancer, choreographer and director. He was born in Prerov in 1902. The pupil of Berger, he joined the Czech National Ballet at the age of twenty-four, and Pavlova's company in the same year. In 1932 Borovansky joined the Ballet Russe de Monte Carlo; he stayed with them six years and then left for Australia, where he opened a school and ballet club from which he developed the Borovansky Ballet at Melbourne.

Borovansky revived all the classical ballets and choreographed many new ones, *Terra Australis*, *Caprizzione Italienne*, *The Black Swan* and *Outlaw*. Borovansky died in Sydney in 1959, leaving Australia a priceless legacy of ballet. In 1960 Peggy van Praagh became Artistic Director of the company, which later became the Australian Ballet.

As a character dancer Borovansky was considered very fine. He created the role of the Strong Man in Massine's *Le Beau Danube* – very different from the Artist in *Le Lion Amoureux*.

18

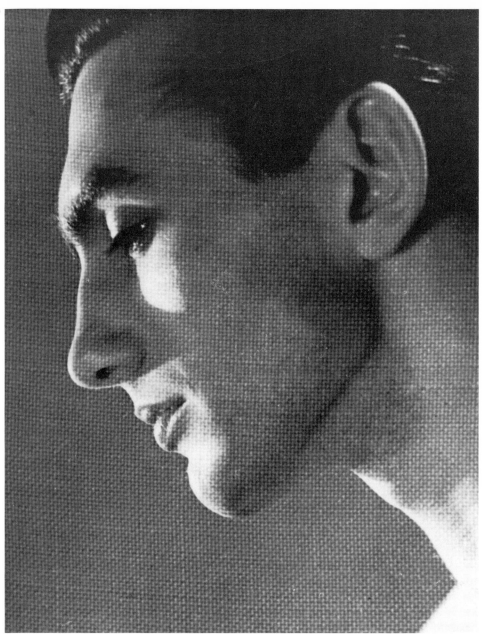

Oleg Briansky   A principal danseur
noble, he was born in Brussels in 1929.
Amongst his teachers were Victor Gsovsky,
Rousanne, Kniaseff and Volkova.

Briansky made his debut in Brussels in
1945, joining Roland Petit's Ballets des
Champs Elysées the following year and
Petit's Ballets de Paris in 1949, leaving them
after a tour of America to form his own
group and to teach.

In 1951 Briansky joined the Festival
Ballet as a principal dancer, staying with
them for four years, during which time he
created the role of Mephisto in Ashton's
Vision of Marguerite. He left them to dance
in the USA, forming his own company and
teaching in New York and at the Saratoga
Ballet Centre.

Janine Charrat   Choreographer, première danseuse, director and teacher. Janine Charrat, who was born in Grenoble in 1924, has been described as a highly dramatic dancer of great art and lyricism. She studied under Egorova and Volinine, making her debut as a child star in the film *La Mort du Cygne* (1937).

Charrat's real career started when she joined Roland Petit's Ballet des Champs Elysées for whom she choreographed several ballets. She joined Lifar's Nouveau Ballet de Monte Carlo in 1946, and he created *Prière* for her. She danced a leading role in Lifar's *Chota Roustaveli* also.

After leaving the Monte Carlo Ballet, Charrat was a guest artist all over France and Germany in most major ballet companies, dancing and choreographing works for them, amongst which were *Adame Miroir*, *Abraxas*, *Jeu de Cartes* and perhaps her most dramatic one *Les Algues*. In 1951 Charrat formed her own company, Ballets de France. She became director of the Geneva Ballet in 1961 and opened her own school of ballet in Paris in 1969 continuing with her choreography. She has been made an Officer of Arts and Letters and was awarded the Légion d'Honneur in 1973.

Alan Carter   English dancer, choreographer and director, was born in London in 1920. He studied with Astafieva Legat and Italia Conti, and the Sadler's Wells Ballet School, becoming a soloist in the Company 1938–41 and created the title role in Ashton's ballet *Harlequin in the Street*.

Alan Carter joined the Sadler's Wells Theatre Ballet in 1946, also making his first essay in choreography, *The Catch*. After a year he left to become a ballet master for films, choreographing the dance sequence for *The Man Who Loved Redheads*, and many others.

In 1948–50 Alan Carter founded and directed the St James' Ballet, and became ballet master for the Empire Theatre. After this he was director of ballets in Munich, for which he choreographed *The Miraculous Mandarin* and *Prince of the Pagodas*. For the Wuppertal company he choreographed *The Sleeping Beauty* and *Swan Lake*, and Shostakovich's tenth Symphony. Since then Carter has directed the ballet companies at Tel Aviv and Istanbul and in Iceland.

William Chappell   English dancer, choreographer, producer and stage designer. A Londoner born in 1908, he studied with Marie Rambert at the Ballet Club, danced with Ida Rubenstein's company and joined the Vic-Wells Ballet as a principal dancer and stage designer in 1931.

A most remarkably gifted man, he often danced principal roles in the ballets for which he did the design and costumes – *The Jar*, *The Judgement of Paris* and *Les Patineurs*. He also created leading roles in other ballets including de Valois's *The Haunted Ballroom*, *The Gods go A'Begging*, *La Création du Monde*, and *The Rake's Progress*, also the Sailor in Ashton's *Rio Grande*.

Chappell designed sets and costumes for *Giselle* in 1935 and for the first full-length *Coppélia* in 1940. He left the Company shortly before the war and continued his career after that by choreographing for, and producing musicals, writing books on ballet and producing plays. A pioneer dancer of the Royal Ballet.

Yvette Chauviré   The Prima Ballerina Assoluta étoile of the Paris Opera Ballet – the Fonteyn of France. Born in France in 1917 of French parents, she trained at the Conservatoire of the Paris Opera from which dancers graduate to the Paris Opera Ballet.

Chauviré was equally popular as a person and as a ballerina, her portrayal of Giselle being considered the finest in France. On her first visit to London with Lifar's Nouveau Ballet de Monte Carlo in 1946 she made a terrific success in *Giselle* and as Princess Daredjan in *Chota Roustaveli* – a role she created for Lifar.

Chauviré spent many years as guest artist on the continent, in America, and in England with the Royal Ballet at Covent Garden in 1958, and despite her retirement from the Paris Opera Ballet in 1958 she was warmly welcomed back by them as guest artist, eventually becoming a director of their Ballet School and of the Académie Internationale de Danse.

Yvette Chauviré was made a Chevalier de la Légion d'Honneur in 1964.

Pauline Clayden was a ballerina of exceptional finesse with an almost fey quality about her work. Born in London in 1922, trained at the Cone-Ripman school, she made her debut with the Covent Garden Opera Ballet, Antony Tudor's London Ballet, and the Ballet Rambert in 1941; she then joined the Sadler's Wells Ballet.

Pauline Clayden quickly became a principal dancer, taking over some of Fonteyn's roles in *Nocturne*, *Daphnis and Chloë*, *Hamlet*, and *The Quest*; also creating roles in Ashton's *Les Sirènes*, and de Valois's *Promenade*. Perhaps her most dramatic creative role was the 'suicide' in Helpmann's *Miracle in the Gorbals*. Her performance in this ballet was a perfect understatement of melodrama, turning it into a work of art and subtlety. Furthermore, to follow the 'magic' of Fonteyn as Chloë was a great challenge, but she wisely did not copy her, and gave to it the child-like quality of fairytale which was most moving.

Pauline Clayden retired in 1956 to become a teacher.

Margaret Dale Dancer, choreograp_her and producer. She was born in Newcastle-upon-Tyne and trained by Nellie Potts and the Sadler's Wells Ballet School. She was a ballerina of wide range, from the Sugar Plum Fairy in *Casse Noisette* to the Widow in *Balabilée*, the Tango in *Façade* and Swanilda in *Coppélia*. She also danced the Bluebird pas de deux in both the Sadlers Wells production of *Sleeping Princess* (1939) and *Sleeping Beauty* (1946).

Margaret Dale joined the Sadler's Wells Ballet in 1938 after dancing in pantomimes, making her debut in de Valois's *Le Roi Nu*. She created roles in several ballets, including *Le Roi Nu*, Roland Petit's *Balabilée*, de Valois's *The Prospect Before Us*, Helpmann's *Comus* and choreographed *The Great Detective* for the Sadler's Wells Theatre Ballet.

Margaret Dale retired in 1954 and made a name for herself producing ballet for television – *Lac des Cygnes*, *Coppélia*, *Casse Noisette*, *Giselle*, *The Sleeping Beauty* and *La Sylphide* and several others. She also made feature films on Pavlova, Karsavina and Marie Rambert.

Margaret Dale left England to continue her career in Canada.

28

Alexandra Danilova One of the best-known and most popular ballerinas of this century. She was born in Peterhof in 1904, studied at the Imperial School and made her debut at the Marinsky. In 1924 Danilova joined the Diaghilev Ballet, attaining the title of ballerina in 1927, and from then on her successes never ceased. She spent nineteen years with the Ballets Russes companies as ballerina during which she created the role of the Serving Maid in *The Gods Go A'Begging* at Covent Garden in 1937. She was guest artist for the Festival Ballet, the Sadler's Wells Ballet, La Scala, and at one time ran her own Company. She mounted ballets for the Met in New York, where she gave her farewell performance in 1957. Amongst her most famous roles are the Street Dancer in *Le Beau Danube* and the Can-Can Dancer in *La Boutique Fantasque*, in which nobody has ever rivalled her vivacity, sparkle and sheer *joie de vivre*.

Amongst the classics Danilova was known to be paramount in *Giselle, The Firebird* and as Swanilda in *Coppélia*. Since her retirement Danilova has become a teacher and lecturer.

32

Anton Dolin Premier danseur, actor, choreographer, author.

Patrick Healey-Kay was born in Slinfold, Sussex, in 1904, and studied with Grace Cone and with Astafieva. Under the name of Patrikieeff he joined the Diaghilev Ballet as a page in *The Sleeping Princess* in 1921, becoming known in 1923 as Anton Dolin and as a premier danseur of virility, versatility, strength and showmanship; on top of all that he had the Irish charm and persuasive powers which proved a great asset in his career.

Dolin has danced everything, with everybody, and everywhere, so details of such a career are impossible in a short space. He founded the Markova-Dolin and London Festival Ballet companies, was premier danseur for both, and did some choreography. He created the first jazz ballet in England to George Gershwin's *Rhapsody in Blue*. He also acted in Christmas plays and published six books on ballet.

Dolin danced in films and musicals, and partnered famous ballerinas from Olga Spessivtseva to a well-known young skater Belita Jepson Turner, dancing the *Bluebird* with her.

Dolin's partnership with Markova, which lasted over thirty years, is in itself legendary.

Perhaps his finest creation of a role was that of Satan in de Valois's ballet of *Job* – a shattering performance of muscular, bombastic, fiendish arrogance – never surpassed. As David in Keith Lester's ballet the strength and vitality were there but the mood in a more gentle mould. In the classical roles Dolin's performances are considered amongst the greatest of all.

There is no doubt whatever that Dolin has done tremendous work in making the male dancer acceptable to everyone. Today Dolin teaches, lectures and is involved in filming.

33

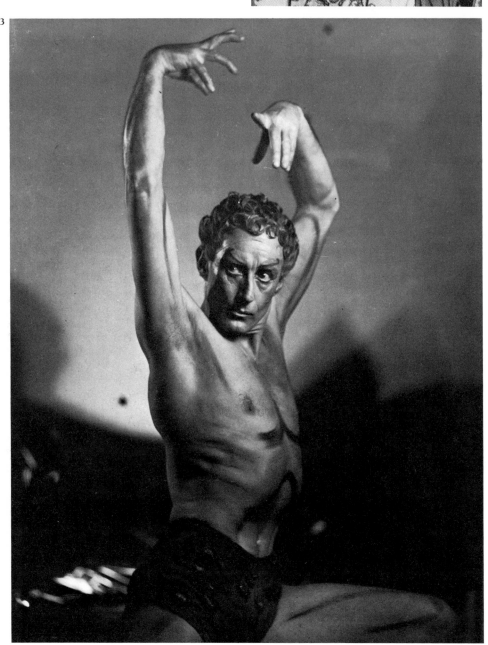

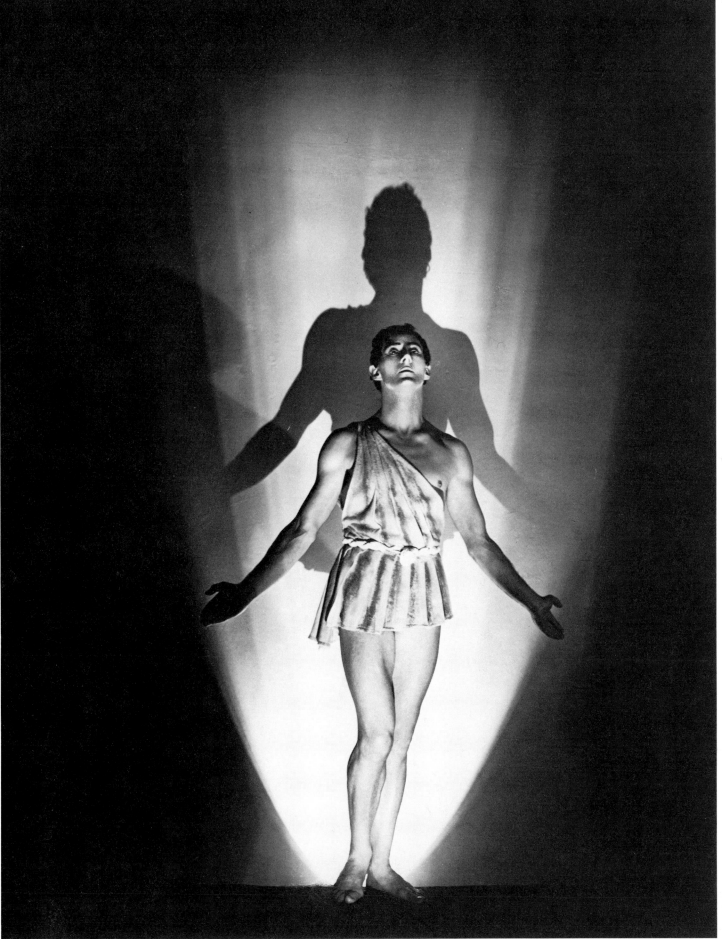

Leslie Edwards English mime and character dancer. Born in Teddington in 1916, he was a protégé of Marie Rambert and soloist in her Company for two years until he joined the Vic-Wells Ballet. He is one of the oldest members of the Royal Ballet having been with them for over forty years, and one of its most faithful and useful members.

. Leslie Edwards has created numerous demi-character roles, varying from his comic portrayal of the Old Farmer in Ashton's *La Fille Mal Gardée*, his ingratiatingly grand and graciously pompous Catalabutte in *The Sleeping Beauty*, the diabolic witchcraft of Archimado in Ashton's *The Quest* and his lovable and doddering old beggar in Helpmann's *Miracle in the Gorbals*, to the stern unbending Bilby in Andrée Howard's *A Mirror for Witches*.

Leslie Edwards was guest teacher and director for the National Ballet of Canada from 1962. He is also founder and director of the Royal Ballet Choreographic Group, and Régisseur for the Royal Ballet.

André Eglevsky Premier danseur noble, he was born in Moscow in 1917, and brought up in France. He was taught dancing first at Nice by Nivelskaya, then in Paris by Egorova, Volinine, Kchessinska, and finally in London by Legat.

Eglevsky made his debut at the age of fourteen with the de Basil Ballets Russes de Monte Carlo which he left to join Léon Woizikowski's ballet. In 1936 he joined the René Blum Ballets de Monte Carlo as a principal dancer for which he created his first leading role in *L'Épreuve d'Amour* in which he made a very great impression especially with his tour de force of slow pirouettes gradually ending on the ground.

In the years to come he became as popular for his dancing in modern works as he was in the classics – a fine golden slave in *Scheherazade*. In modern ballet he danced many roles including those in *Mam'zelle Angot* for Massine, *Apollo* and *The Scotch Symphony* for Balanchine, and as Paris in *Helen of Troy*. For the Ballet International of New York Eglevsky choreographed *Colloque Sentimentale* with decor by Salvador Dali.

Eglevsky taught at the School of American Ballet, later opening his own school and company in Massapequa on Long Island. He died in 1977.

Richard Ellis   English demi-character
dancer. He joined the Vic-Wells Ballet from
the School in 1933 as a soloist, remaining
with the Sadler's Wells Ballet and the Royal
Ballet with a break in the war for service in
the Navy, until his retirement as a dancer.

Richard Ellis created the role of the
Birdcatcher in Ashton's *Harlequin in the
Street* and the debonaire Captain of the
Guard in Massine's *Mam'zelle Angot*. He
also took over the role of the Friend in de
Valois's *Rake's Progress* and the Shepherd
in her *Gods Go A'Begging*.

In 1947 Richard Ellis married Christine
du Boulay (also in the Company) and retired
from the Royal Ballet with her to America,
where they opened a school of ballet.

Julia Farron Born as Joyce Farron-Smith in London in 1922, she was a demi-character ballerina of classical technique, and a fine actress and teacher.

Julia Farron won a scholarship from the Cone School into the Vic-Wells Ballet School in 1934, and made her debut with the Company in 1936 in de Valois's *Nursery Suite*. Her first important creation was as Pepe, the dog, in Ashton's *A Wedding Bouquet* in 1937.

Both as a dancer and as an actress Farron created roles and danced the lead in many ballets – her best known dancing roles were as Psyche in Ashton's *Cupid and Psyche*, Belle Epine in Cranko's *Prince of the Pagodas*, Alicia in de Valois's *The Haunted Ballroom* and the Red Queen in de Valois's *Checkmate*. As an actress – Carabosse and the Queen in *Sleeping Beauty*, the Prostitute in Helpmann's *Miracle in the Gorbals*, and last of all, as Lady Capulet in MacMillan's *Romeo and Juliet*.

Julia Farron retired in 1961 to teach at the Royal Ballet School, but has frequently returned to Covent Garden as a guest artist.

41

Violetta Elvin Born in Moscow in 1924 as Violetta Prokhorova, she was a pupil of Vaganova at the Bolshoi School from which she made her debut at the State Theatre in Tashkent, returning to dance as a soloist for the Bolshoi Ballet. Violetta came to England in 1946 shortly after changing her name by marriage to Violetta Elvin, and she brought a first taste of the Bolshoi School of Ballet – her Bluebird was one of the sensations of *The Sleeping Beauty* at her first performance with us.

Violetta Elvin was lovely in every way, personality, looks and character, and had impeccable technique. During her stay with the Sadler's Wells Ballet she danced nearly all the classical roles and created some modern ones including Lykanion in Ashton's *Daphnis and Chloë* and Water in *Homage to the Queen*. Violetta Elvin was guest artist in South America, Stockholm and Italy. She also appeared in several films. A radiant and charming aura set off her dramatic and ethereal qualities in *Giselle*.

This ballerina, who was as popular with her audiences as with her colleagues, retired in 1956 with a memorable performance of Aurora in *The Sleeping Beauty*, to remarry and live in Italy.

John Field Danseur noble and teacher. He was born in Doncaster in 1921, where he trained as a dancer with Shelagh Elliott-Clarke and Edna Slocombe. He made his debut with the Vic-Wells Ballet in 1939.

John Field soon became a principal classical dancer of the Company – partnering Svetlana Beriosova and Violetta Elvin, and he was Beryl Grey's principal partner. They appeared in the first stereoscopic ballet film *The Black Swan* in 1952. He has danced the leading roles in most of the classics and created the role of Dorkon in Ashton's *Daphnis and Chloë*.

John Field has been a director of Sadler's Wells Theatre Ballet, the Touring Company, and assistant director of the Royal Ballet of Covent Garden. He has also directed ballet at La Scala and for the South Carolina Ballet Company.

John Field retired from the Royal Ballet in 1971. He received the CBE in 1967, and was director of the Royal Academy of Dancing. In 1979 he became artistic director of London Festival Ballet.

Elaine Fifield A ballerina of infinite qualities both as dancer and actress, she was born in Sydney, Australia, in 1930.

At the age of fifteen Fifield won a Royal Academy of Dancing scholarship, joining the Sadler's Wells Theatre Ballet as a soloist in 1947. She was very soon promoted to a principal dancer. In 1954 Fifield joined the Sadler's Wells Ballet, 'the parent company' at Covent Garden, becoming a prima ballerina in 1956. She danced the title roles in the classics, including *Lac des Cygnes* and *Coppélia*, and created the leading roles in Ashton's *Madame Chrysanthème* and Cranko's *Pineapple Poll*. Nothing could be more diverse than those four leading roles, which proves her remarkable range of characterization, for with all her vitality and gaiety Fifield could still be a lovely and moving Odette. It is sad that one never saw enough of her – for she retired in 1959, but she did emerge in 1964 to join the Australian Ballet. In 1967 she wrote her autobiography, *In My Shoes*.

Michael Fokine Choreographer, premier danseur and teacher. He was born in 1880 in St Petersburg and trained there, joining the Marinsky in 1898 as soloist, started teaching in 1902, became a principal soloist in 1904, he created his first ballet in 1905, *Acis and Galatea*. He died in 1942.

Fokine was already known as a premier danseur when he left Russia to join Diaghilev in 1909. He took this action as he disapproved of the 'ancient' methods of producing ballets, having decided that ballet should be a complete union between music, design and choreography. His *Les Sylphides* is considered to be the forerunner of Massine's symphonic ballets.

Fokine's works are legion – the most famous being *Le Spectre de la Rose*, *Scheherazade*, *Le Coq d'Or*, *Carnaval*, *Petrouchka* and *The Firebird* – latterly *Paganini* and *L'Épreuve d'Amour*. He might accurately be described as the pioneer of modern choreography.

Frederic Franklin English premier danseur. Born in Liverpool in 1914, he was a demi-character dancer from the Elliott-Clarke and Legat ballet schools. His career was in musicals until he joined the Markova-Dolin Company as a principal dancer in 1935.

In 1938 Franklin joined the Ballet Russe de Monte Carlo as a principal dancer, creating a leading role in Massine's *Seventh Symphony*, the Baron in Massine's *Gaîté Parisienne*, and dancing the Warrior in Fokine's *Prince Igor*, before becoming a maître de ballet of the Company in 1944.

In 1949 Franklin was a guest artist for the Sadler's Wells Ballet at Covent Garden in *Coppélia* with Danilova and partnered Markova in *Les Sylphides* in 1950. He became co-ordinator of the Washington Civic Ballet in 1959 and Artistic Adviser for the American Ballet Theatre in 1961. In 1962 he worked at La Scala, and became Director of the Washington National Ballet and School.

Margot Fonteyn A legend in her time and, at the peak of her career, considered the finest prima ballerina in the world.

Margot Fonteyn was born Peggy Hookham, in Reigate in 1919 of English parents. She was trained by Bosustow, Goncharov, Astafieva, and the Sadler's Wells Ballet School in 1934. Within one year of joining the School she made her debut in the corps de ballet of the Company and in 1935 had her first leading role as the Creole Girl in *Rio Grande*. She became a ballerina of the Company in 1936 and danced her first full-length *Giselle* at the age of eighteen; this was followed by all the great classical roles, as well as creating leading roles in most of Ashton's ballets.

Margot Fonteyn has been guest artist in most of the great opera houses in the world and is greatly responsible for the popularity of ballet today. I will mention but a few of the ballets in which she created roles – *Apparitions, Ondine, Daphnis and Chloë, Marguerite and Armand, Symphonic Variations*, among Ashton's ballets; she excelled in the classics of *Coppélia, Giselle, Casse Noisette, Le Lac des Cygnes*, and greatest of all her Aurora in *The Sleeping Beauty*, for which, in 1946, she received a 'ticker-tape' reception in New York recorded in the world's press.

In 1951 Margot Fonteyn was awarded the CBE, and she became a Dame of the British Empire in 1956. At the age of sixty Dame Margot dances very little, but when she does that 'magic' still works. It may also be the reason for her 'enigmatic' character, a mixture of gold and quicksilver. Many books have been published on Dame Margot Fonteyn. She published her autobiography in 1975 and *The Magic of Dance* in 1980.

Dame Margot Fonteyn still lives and works for her art – and other people. She is President of the Royal Academy of Dancing.

Celia Franca (left)   A dramatic demi-character dancer, choreographer, founder and director of the National Ballet of Canada.

Born in London in 1921 of English parents, Celia Franca studied with the Royal Academy of Dancing, Marie Rambert, Antony Tudor, and Idzikowski. She made her debut with the Ballet Rambert in 1937, then joined Sadler's Wells Ballet in 1941. For them she danced leading roles, and created the Queen in *Hamlet*, the Prostitute in Helpmann's *Miracle in the Gorbals*, and the spider in *The Spider's Banquet*. She choreographed *Khadra* and *Bailemos* for the Sadler's Wells Theatre Ballet.

In 1951 Celia Franca left for Canada to found the Canadian Ballet. She started with only a small group of dancers and specialized in the reproduction of all the classical ballets – she herself had been the first truly dramatically compelling Queen of the Wilis with the Sadler's Wells Ballet in 1941 with her strong imperious movements and lovely elevation. The Company toured the USA twice and first travelled to England in 1972. It opened its own school in 1959. Celia Franca reached the peak of her career as director when she commissioned Rudolf Nureyev to produce the full-length *Sleeping Beauty* for them in 1973 in which he toured the USA. Celia Franca retired in 1974.

Sally Gilmour   A dancer of surpassing acting abilities. She was born in Malaya in 1921, studied in Singapore and with Karsavina, before joining Marie Rambert's School. In a very short time she graduated into the Ballet Rambert and became a star.

Sally Gilmour created many roles for the company, the most important of which were Mrs Tebrick in *Lady into Fox*, *Confessional* and Tulip in *The Sailor's Return*. A demi-character dancer, she was acknowledged to be the 'greatest dramatic dancer of her generation' equally good in a humorous role such as the Duck in *Peter and the Wolf* as she was in *The Fugitive*.

Although technically not strong as a classical dancer, Sally Gilmour received great laudatory acclaim from the press for her sensitive and dramatic rendering of the title role in *Giselle*.

Sally Gilmour married and left to live in Australia in 1953, coming back to England in 1972. She now teaches dancing in London.

John Gilpin   A popular English premier danseur of the forties and fifties.

John Gilpin was born in Southsea in 1930, and appeared as a child actor until he started taking dancing lessons with the Cone-Ripman and Marie Rambert Schools. He made his debut with the Rambert Ballet in 1945 and toured Australia with them as a premier danseur.

In 1949 Gilpin joined Roland Petit's Les Ballets de Paris as a principal dancer creating the leading role in *Le Rève de Leonor,* but it was not until he joined the Festival Ballet in 1950 that he became accepted as one of our greatest classical male dancers. One of Gilpin's greatest successes in modern ballet was in Jack Carter's ballet of *The Witch Boy* in which his training as an actor came to the fore. His tremendous technique was particularly dazzling in Harald Lander's *Etudes.*

Gilpin left the Festival Ballet to be a guest artist, both in Europe and America, partnering many of the famous ballerinas of the period. He returned as guest artist to the Festival Ballet, before retiring in 1970 to become a teacher of dancing.

63

6

Nana Gollner An American classical prima ballerina noted for her beauty, technical virtuosity and the lovely fluidity of her line.

Nana Gollner was born in El Paso in 1920 and trained with Kosloff in Paris. She first danced leads in London with Blum's Ballets de Monte Carlo and made a great impression with her performance as Odette in *Le Lac des Cygnes*, similarly when she danced Swanilda in *Coppélia* with the International Ballet.

Nana Gollner has danced in Paramount films and for Reinhardt in Los Angeles for his production of *A Midsummer's Night's Dream*. She has been prima ballerina for many companies: American Ballet Theatre, de Basil's Ballets Russes de Monte Carlo, and Mona Inglesby's International Ballet.

Paul Petroff Danish premier danseur noble. He was born in Elsinore 1908 and studied dancing in Copenhagen. He joined Colonel de Basil's Ballets Russes de Monte Carlo as a premier danseur in 1932 and worked with them for eleven years. One of the mainstays of the Company, he would take any role and was always certain to give a 'performance', with his pleasing personality and neat Danish technique. The most notable role he created was that of Paolo in *Francesca da Rimini*, which David Lichine created specially for him and Lubov Tchernicheva. Others were in *Les Présages*, *Choreartium* and the Prince in Fokine's *Cendrillon*.

When Petroff left the de Basil Company he joined the American Ballet Theatre for two years as a principal dancer. He and his wife Nana Gollner joined the International Ballet as guest stars for a season during which they danced *Coppélia* in a 'delightfully gay and spirited way'. They then left for America.

Ram Gopal. Internationally known as one of the finest exponents and teacher of pure classical Indian dance drama, Ram Gopal first came to England in 1939 at the Aldwych Theatre. He returned in 1951, doing much to create an understanding and appreciation of Indian dancing and cultural art in the Western world.

Ram Gopal was born in Bangalore in 1920, and studied with four of the most famous teachers of classical dancing. In 1944 he won the prize at the All-Indian Dance Festival in Bombay, having already opened his school of dancing in Bangalore in 1935, at which he had taught Mrinalini Sarabhai, herself now a star of international fame.

Alexander Grant One of the greatest demi-character dancers of this century. He was born in Wellington, New Zealand in 1925, won a scholarship from the Royal Academy of Dancing to the Sadler's Wells Ballet School and within two years made his debut as a soloist with the Company at Covent Garden, in Ashton's ballet *Les Sirènes*.

Grant created many leading roles in Ashton ballets, including *Ondine, Enigma Variations, Bonne Bouche, A Month in the Country*, and in *La Fille Mal Gardée*. As Alain in the last of these (the old farmer's comic son) he has never been bettered – whimsical, moving and outrageously funny – a fine dancer and great artist.

Alexander Grant became director of the Royal Ballet Group of Ballet for All in 1971 but continued with his dancing, and in 1976 he became director of the National Ballet of Canada with which he still occasionally dances the role of Carabosse in *Sleeping Beauty*. He received the CBE in 1965.

Tamara Grigorieva   Director, dancer and ballet mistress. The lovely daughter-in-law of Lubov Tchernicheva, she was born in Petrograd in 1918, studied with Preobrajenska, Vilzak, and Balanchine in whose company Les Ballets 1933 she made her debut as a soloist, joining the de Basil Ballets Russes Company in the same year as a principal dancer.

In the 1938 de Basil season at Covent Garden Grigorieva 'inherited' Tchernicheva's role in Lichine's *Francesca da Rimini*, after which she settled in Rio de Janeiro at the Teatro Municipal for two years. She rejoined de Basil in 1940 and later became guest ballerina at the Colón Theatre in Buenos Aires, then ballet mistress and director of the Montevideo Ballet, eventually becoming ballet mistress and director of the Colón Theatre in 1956.

Beryl Grey Ballerina, authoress, and former artistic director of the Festival Ballet, she was one of the finest ballerinas of the century.

Beryl Grey was born in London in 1927. She studied at the Sadler's Wells Ballet School at the age of nine, later entering the Company itself, and within five years became a soloist. At the age of fourteen Beryl Grey danced her first full-length *Lac des Cygnes* and danced *Giselle* a year later.

Beryl Grey danced all the leading roles in the classics during her sixteen years with the Company; she also danced and created leading roles in modern ballets including Massine's *Donald of the Burthens*, Ashton's *The Quest* and de Valois's *Don Quixote*.

In 1952 Beryl Grey made the first stereoscopic ballet film – *The Black Swan*. She has been a guest artist in Sweden, New Zealand, South Africa, Australia, for the Peking Ballet Company, and for the Bolshoi and the Marinsky Theatres, after which she wrote two books, *Through the Bamboo Curtain* and *Red Curtain Up*.

Beryl Grey was Artistic Director of London Festival Ballet from 1968 until 1979 when she became Vice-Patron of the Company. She was awarded the CBE in 1971.

Gordon Hamilton   A character dancer. He was born in Sydney, Australia in 1918, and studied under Lubov Egorova, joining her Ballet de la Jeunesse in 1937, the Ballet Rambert and the Anglo-Polish Ballet from 1938 to 1940 when he joined the Sadler's Wells Ballet as a principal dancer. He created the role of the Lepidopterist in de Valois's ballet *Promenade* in 1943, in which he was dotty and crazily delightful as the old man with his butterfly net, and as Mr Taylor, a role he took over from Claude Newman, in de Valois's *The Prospect Before Us*, he certainly equalled, if not superseded, the creator.

Gordon Hamilton really had the 'wanderlust' in a big way. He never seemed to stay put. After leaving the Sadler's Wells Ballet he joined Roland Petit's Ballets des Champs Elysées (on and off) for which he created the role of the Witch in *La Sylphide* in 1951. He left to do musicals in America, returning to Europe in 1954 to become ballet master for the Vienna State Ballet with much success, and producing *Giselle* for them in 1955. He died in Paris in 1959.

John Hart Premier danseur. Born in London in 1921, he was trained by Judith Espinosa and won the gold medal of the Royal Academy of Dancing. He joined the Vic-Wells Ballet in 1938 and rapidly made a name for himself as dancer and actor, the latter shown in his roles as Orion in Ashton's *Sylvia*, Laertes in Helpmann's *Hamlet*, and the Official in Helpmann's *Miracle in the Gorbals*. For many years he was one of the mainstays of the Company – nothing could be further apart than the comic Corregidor in Massine's *Tricorne* and Albrecht in *Giselle* – a fine dancer with remarkable range.

In 1955 Hart became ballet master for the Sadler's Wells Ballet – and later assistant director of the Royal Ballet. He was a Director of the International University of Performing Arts in San Diego, and Administrator of the Royal Ballet for two years. In 1971 John Hart was awarded the CBE.

Robert Helpmann 'A Man for All Theatres'. Born in Mount Gambier, Australia, Robert Helpmann started his career with Pavlova and Novikoff. Premier danseur noble, choreographer, actor, director and producer, he joined the Vic-Wells (1933 until 1950) as premier danseur. His partnership with Margot Fonteyn was famous.

Helpmann created many roles for the Company; amongst the best known were: for de Valois – the Red King in *Checkmate*, Prometheus in *Prometheus*, Mr O'Reilly in *The Prospect Before Us* and Orpheus in *Orpheus and Eurydice*; for Ashton – the Poet in *Apparitions*, the young man in *Nocturne*, the leader of the children of darkness in *Dante Sonata* and an ugly sister in *Cinderella*.

Helpmann also choreographed and danced the leads in *Comus*, *Hamlet*, *Miracle in the Gorbals* and *Adam Zero*.

Like Fonteyn, Helpmann is a legend in his own lifetime. He created the role of Prince Florimund in the companies first production of *The Sleeping Princess* (*Sleeping Beauty*) in 1939, and again at Covent Garden in 1946 when he created ballet history by doubling the roles of Carabosse and Prince Florimund.

Helpmann could out-clown Grimaldi (he too was a dancer) and had a highly developed sense of drama often bordering on the macabre.

Since retiring from the Royal Ballet, Robert Helpmann has concentrated on The Australian Ballet with Dame Peggy van Praagh, producing and directing, and has choreographed ballets for them. He was awarded the CBE, in 1964 and was knighted in 1968.

Mary Honer English virtuoso ballerina
and teacher. She was born in London in
1914 and trained under Judith Espinosa,
Margaret Craske and Legat.

Mary Honer spent her early years dancing
in pantomimes and musicals until she
joined the Vic-Wells Ballet in 1936 as a
principal ballerina, remaining with them
until she retired in 1942. In the early years
of the Company she was a tower of strength
with her technical qualities in leading roles
of the classics – *Casse Noisette*, *Lac des
Cygnes* and *Coppélia*, and created roles in
modern ballet for Ashton and de Valois, of
which the most witty and sparkling was
the bride in Ashton's *A Wedding Bouquet*
and for sheer technical virtuosity as one of
the two girls in blue in Ashton's *Les
Patineurs* – she was particularly noted for
her *fouettés* in the third act of *Lac des
Cygnes*.

Mary Honer retired in 1942 to become an
actress and opened a school of ballet in
London. She died in 1965.

Mona Inglesby English dancer, choreographer, founder director and prima ballerina of the International Ballet 1940–53. Mona Inglesby trained under Margaret Craske, Marie Rambert and Lubov Egorova. Before founding her company she danced for Marie Rambert and the Russian Ballet at Covent Garden in 1939. Mona Inglesby's company toured the provinces during the war mainly with productions of the classics – *Swan Lake*, *Giselle, Coppélia* and the *Sleeping Beauty* – apart from her own works of *Comus, Endymion, Amoras, Everyman* and others, doing fine pioneering work in bringing ballet to a wider public by appearing in the super cinemas – as the Royal Ballet does with the Big Tops today. Stanislas Idzikowski was her teacher and ballet master. Nicholas Serguéeff, régisseur general, produced the classics and many well-known dancers appeared with the Company, including Nana Gollner, Paul Petroff, Nina Tarakanova, Harold Turner, and Hélène Armfelt. Maurice Béjart and Moira Shearer made their debuts in her company, which was particularly known for its 'luscious' productions giving much well-earned relaxation to war-wearied workers!

90

Renée Jeanmaire Known to her friends and compatriots as Zizi, a perfect nickname, as her 'life' seems to flow through her body with the sparkle of champagne (the best!) in her eyes.

Jeanmaire was born in Paris in 1924, studied at the Opera School and made her debut with the Opera Ballet, leaving them to give recitals. Then she started her career in earnest, dancing with Roland Petit and subsequently joined Lifar's Nouveau Ballet de Monte Carlo as a soloist. She joined the de Basil company, then left and had her first important roles as ballerina with Roland Petit's Ballets de Paris in 1948. She created what became the most popular role of her life in Roland Petit's brilliant *Carmen* in which her acting was breathtaking – her vitality and wildcat viciousness were positively alarming – dance drama at its highest level. Shortly after she left to dance in musicals and films in America.

In her Aurora pas de deux with Vladimir Skouratoff she performed in the 'grand manner', dancing with brilliance, in *Piccoli* she was all 'pizzicato', gaiety and Parisienne piquancy – truly a 'diamond of the dance' with many facets.

Kurt Jooss Dancer, choreographer, founder and director of the Ballets Jooss. Born in Wasseralfingen in 1901, he studied dancing and music with Rudolph von Laban, founder of the Central European School of Dancing.

In 1924 Jooss formed the Neue Tanzbühne at the Munster Theatre with Sigurd Leeder, the lovely Aino Siimola (she later became his wife and taught at the school), Frederic Cohen, the musical director, and Hein Heckroth, the scenic and costume designer. They produced several ballets for that theatre. In 1927 Jooss founded the Folkwang Schule at Essen of which he was the director, later becoming Master of Ballet at the Essen Opera House. In 1932 he won the competition of the Archives Internationales de la Danse with *The Green Table* (still being reproduced today) and started his famous world tours with his Ballets Jooss.

Jooss's output was prolific but his most popular works were dramatic: *The Green Table, Chronica, The Big City, The Prodigal Son*, and *Seven Heroes*.

Kurt Jooss's ballets were mainly of political implications and 'strong meat' – dance drama based upon the Central European School of Dancing. His works seemed to me 'a cry for peace' in the wilderness of the world's political rottenness. A man of great charm and gentleness without weakness – it was a pity that war deprived us of the works of this fine choreographer and humanist.

Alexandre Kalioujny   Character dancer.
Born in Prague in 1923, he studied under
Preobrajenska in Paris, and made his debut
with the Ballet de Cannes in Paris in 1946
and his London debut the same year with
Serge Lifar's Nouveau Ballet de Monte
Carlo at the Cambridge Theatre, electrifying
English audiences with his performance as
the Golden Slave in *Scheherazade*.

   In 1947 Kalioujny became a danseur étoile
of the Paris Opera under the direction of
Lifar, until he left for America to dance in
musicals. He returned to the Paris Opera
Ballet in 1956 again as étoile and retired in
1961 to teach in Nice.

Nora Kaye   Considered one of the finest dramatic actress ballerinas of her time. Like all well-trained classical dancers she was equally happy in the classics as in modern ballet, but her greatest successes were in Antony Tudor's *Pillar of Fire* and Agnes de Mille's *Fall River Legend*.

Nora Kaye was born in New York in 1920 as Nora Koreff of Russian parents. She had her early training with the New York Metropolitan Opera Ballet Company School. Amongst her teachers were Fokine, Vilzak, Tudor and Margaret Craske. She made her debut at the Metropolitan Opera as a child

and was an original member of Ballet Theatre, dancing the title role in *Giselle* for them in 1940, perhaps her greatest success in classical ballet. In 1951 she joined the New York City Ballet, returning to Ballet Theatre in 1954.

Perhaps Nora Kaye's greatest achievement in modern ballet was in the aforementioned ballet of Agnes de Mille's, *Fall River Legend* for Ballet Theatre in 1948. For such roles as these she has been described as 'The Duse of the Dance'; under this well-merited accolade she married and retired in 1961.

John Kriza (right)   Born in Berwyn, Illinois in 1919, he arrived in England as principal dancer with the first visit of the American Ballet Theatre at the Royal Opera House Covent Garden. They certainly brought the breeze of the American prairies with them, and their ballets such as *Fancy Free* were exhilarating for us, and a pleasant change.

'Johnnie' Kriza was a young and popular member of the Company both on and off stage; his best known creations being as one of the sailors in *Fancy Free* and in *Interplay*, our first introduction to the choreographic work of Jerome Robbins.

Kriza was trained by Bentley Stone, Dolin and Tudor – he retired in 1966 but became an assistant director in the Company. He died in 1975 in a drowning accident in Florida.

Michael Kidd   American dancer and choreographer. He was born in New York in 1919, and was trained in the Russian School of Ballet by Ludmilla Schollar and Vilzak. He joined the Ballet Caravan at the age of eighteen, then he joined the Ballet Theatre in 1942 as soloist and later a principal dancer of the Company until 1947.

Michael Kidd choreographed *On Stage* for Ballet Theatre, dancing the leading role as the Handyman – a Chaplinesque type with irrepressible cheerfulness – he also danced the Puppet in *Petrouchka* – a beautifully balanced performance between humanity and puppetry.

Gerd Larsen Nobody could be more typical of her native country, Norway, with her silky corn-coloured hair, fine facial bone structure, plus a touch of the 'northern lights' in her personality. Born in Oslo in 1921, she trained under Margaret Craske and became a member of Antony Tudor's London Ballet from 1938 until 1941, when she joined Mona Inglesby's International Ballet.

In 1944 Gerd Larsen joined the Sadler's Wells Ballet Company as a soloist – she danced two roles in the *Sleeping Beauty*, the Queen and the Fairy of the Crystal Fountain. She excelled in character roles and years later I saw her as the nurse in *Romeo and Juliet*, which to my mind was a gem of characterization – a saucy, lovable type of old nurse, fussed and distressed by the wayward behaviour of her loved charge and at the same time enjoying the intrigue.

After thirty-five years, Gerd Larsen is still with the Royal Ballet, acting and teaching. A highly successful career and still going strong.

Hugh Laing. A danseur noble noted as much for his handsome appearance as for his highly developed, romantic and dramatic performances.

Born in Barbados in 1911, Hugh Laing trained under Margaret Craske, Preobrajenska and Marie Rambert, for whom he created many roles at her Ballet Club, perhaps the most notable of which was as the young lover in Antony Tudor's *Jardin aux Lilas* in 1936. In 1938 Hugh Laing joined Antony Tudor's London Ballet as principal dancer, leaving with Tudor in 1939 to join Ballet Theatre in America, where Tudor created further leading roles for him in his ballets including *Pillar of Fire* and *Romeo and Juliet*. 1950 was to see Hugh Laing add further successes to his career with the New York City Ballet for which he created roles in Tudor's *La Dame aux Camélias*, *La Gloire* and in Bolender's *Miraculous Mandarin*.

Hugh Laing retired from the New York City Ballet to become a successful fashion photographer.

100

Yura Lazowski Polish character dancer of unusual agility and vitality. Born in Warsaw in 1917, he studied at the Opera Ballet School. He came to London with de Basil's Ballets Russes in 1935 and astounded the audiences with the variety of his characterizations in such diverse roles as the Jailor in Massine's *Symphonie Fantastique*, the Waiter in *The Good Humoured Ladies*, the Dandy in *Le Beau Danube*, and his magnificent dancing in *Prince Igor* as a Polovtsian Warrior.

Lazowski has been a sad loss to us in Britain for he has concentrated on working in America. He has now retired and guest-teaches in New York schools.

Serge Lifar (Right) Premier danseur, choreographer, impresario, director and author.

Born in Kiev in 1905. In 1923 Lifar joined the Diaghilev Ballet – within two years he had become premier danseur and choreographer. He was incredibly handsome, had a fine physique and great charm with a touchingly child-like wish to be 'liked'! After Diaghilev's death in 1929 Lifar became premier danseur of the Paris Opera Ballet, which had fallen on its 'Victorian knees' both choreographically and artistically. By 1933 Lifar had been made Professor of the Dance and Director. In 1939 Lifar joined the Ballet Russe de Monte Carlo at Covent Garden where he danced his own *Icare* and Albrecht in *Giselle* with Markova. Despite being past his prime, in both ballets he gave dramatic and moving performances.

During Lifar's directorship of the Paris Opera Ballet, lasting over twenty years, he completely re-organized the establishment, modernizing the teaching system and replacing the Italian school of teaching with the more modern Russian one. As well as being the premier danseur, Lifar did 90 per cent of the choreography, dancing the leading roles himself.

A dynamic person and as controversial as his own ballet of *Icare*, Serge Lifar was the author of eight books on dancing and dancers, and wrote his autobiography, *Ma Vie*, in 1965.

Henry Legerton Born in Melbourne, Australia, in 1917. Dancer, and now Régisseur for the Royal Ballet. He started his career training under Hèléne Kirsova in Australia and with Idzikowski and Vera Volkova in England. He was in the Australian Army during the war, after which he returned to London and joined the Sadler's Wells Ballet in 1946. He was chosen by Massine for the role of the shop assistant in *La Boutique Fantasque* when he revived the ballet at Covent Garden in 1947, with which company he created the role of the Barber in *Don Quixote* for de Valois.

In 1957 Legerton went on tour with the Royal Ballet Touring Company, as a principal dancer and ballet master, during which time he danced the Rake in de Valois's *The Rake's Progress*, Dr Coppelius in *Coppélia* and Carabosse in *Sleeping Beauty*.

108

Catherine Littlefield Dancer, choreographer, founder and Director of the Philadelphia Ballet Company in 1935.

Catherine Littlefield was born in Philadelphia in 1905 and trained there together with her sister **Dorothie**. She was the premiere danseuse of the company with which she toured America for two years.

In 1937 the company went to Paris at the Théâtre des Champs Elysées and on to London in the same year. Apart from her company Catherine Littlefield had choreographed scenes for Sonja Henie in *Ice Revues*. Her most popular works were *Barn Dance* and *Terminal* – the former based on American folk dancing, and the latter 'goings on' at a railway station.

Apart from being the first American company to tour abroad, Catherine Littlefield's company was also the first from America to produce *The Sleeping Beauty*. She died in 1951.

109

Alicia Markova The first internationally famous British ballerina assoluta. Born in London in 1910, she studied under Astafieva, Cecchetti, and Legat before joining Diaghilev's ballet at the age of fifteen – first of a line of baby ballerinas. After his death in 1929 she continued her star-spangled career, dancing for the Camargo Society, Marie Rambert Ballet Club, and the Vic-Wells Ballet, where in 1934 Ninette de Valois had the two great classics *Le Lac des Cygnes* and *Giselle* produced for her by Nicholas Serguéeff during which she earned the title 'assoluta'. She left them to form the Markova-Dolin Company (1935–38), which was re-formed in USA (1945–48). I doubt if there is any national or other ballet company of which Markova has not been a guest artist. There have been many books about her, including two photographic ones of mine (1935 and 1951), *Markova* by Arnold Haskell, and her own *Giselle and I* (1960).

Both by her own art and her ballet company Markova did much to popularize ballet in the USA throughout the war. She was awarded the CBE in 1958 and created a Dame of the British Empire in 1963. Markova holds many honorary university degrees and on her retirement in 1962 she became director of the Opera Ballets at the Metropolitan Opera House, New York, a position she held until 1969.

Markova will remain in the history of ballet as Queen of the 'Ballet Blanc'. Indeed, watching her in *Sylphides* and *Giselle* I have often had the uncanny feeling that she may be the reincarnation of Taglioni.

114

Leonide Massine Danseur, choreographer, ballet master, director and teacher. Leonide Fedorovich Myasin was born in Moscow in 1885, studied at the Imperial School and became one of the great choreographers of this century. Massine made his debut with Diaghilev who hoped he would follow in Nijinsky's footsteps. In 1914 Massine had his first big chance in *The Legend of Joseph*, his success proved Diaghilev to be right. Some years later he created his first ballet *Soleil de Nuit*, after which he continued from one success to another both as a dancer and as a choreographer.

It is impossible to give a fair picture of any great artist's works in a few lines; it is enough to give the names of the most popular of his choreographic works: *Les Femmes de Bonne Humeur, La Boutique Fantasque, Le Tricorne, Le Sacre du Printemps, Les Matelots, Le Pas d'Acier* for Diaghilev.

In 1932, after a short stay choreographing and dancing in ballets for the Roxy Theatre in New York, Massine joined the Ballet Russe de Monte Carlo, for which he choreographed many more works including the controversial symphonic ballets *Les Présages, Choreartium*, and the *Symphonie Fantastique*.

Massine's output was prolific, and there is no country or company he has not worked for, including films and musicals; in 1960 he formed a Company, Balletto Europeo.

In 1969 Massine became a guest teacher of choreography for the Royal Ballet School and wrote his memoirs in the same year – *My Life in Ballet*. He died in 1979.

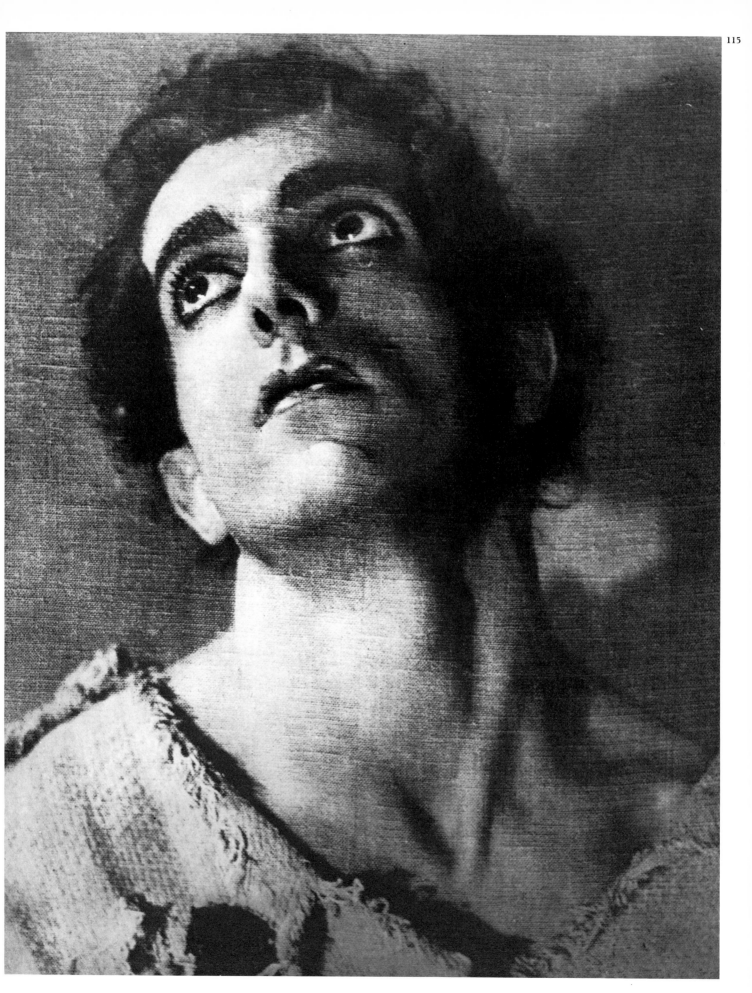

Pamela May   A popular English classical ballerina of the Royal Ballet from its inception as The Vic-Wells Ballet. Born in Trinidad of English parents in 1917, she studied ballet with Freda Grant, Russians in Paris, and Sadler's Wells Ballet School.

In 1933 Pamela May made her debut with the Vic-Wells Ballet, becoming a soloist in 1934. Eventually she became a principal dancer, sharing roles with Margot Fonteyn in the classics, and, in 1946, was one of the Auroras in *The Sleeping Beauty* at Covent Garden, where she also danced Swanilda in *Coppélia*.

During her twenty years with the Royal Ballet Pamela May created roles in five Ashton ballets, four by de Valois and one by John Cranko. Her best-remembered creations are the Red Queen in de Valois's *Checkmate*, Mademoiselle Théodore in de Valois's *The Prospect Before Us*, the Edwardian Mother in Cranko's *Bonne Bouche* Eurydice in de Valois's *Orpheus and Eurydice*, and Ashton's *Symphonic Variations*; all of which were entirely different in mood and style.

Shortly before her retirement from dancing in 1952 Pamela May danced the Can-Can in *La Boutique Fantasque* and Swanilda in *Coppélia*, after which she appeared as guest artist at La Scala and with the Royal Ballet. In 1954 she became a member of the teaching staff at the School until her retirement in 1977.

Elizabeth Miller   English demi-character ballerina. She made her debut with the Vic-Wells Ballet in 1934 in the pas de trois from *Le Lac des Cygnes* with Pamela May and Walter Gore. (It had earlier been danced by Markova, Idzikovski and de Valois.)

Elizabeth Miller was a blonde, petite, and vivacious dancer, both technically and temperamentally suited to the leading roles that she danced: Swanilda (*Coppélia*), Columbine (*Carnaval*), Leo (*Horoscope*), the Girl (*The Rake's Progress*). Her solo as the Fairy of the Song Birds in *The Sleeping Princess* was danced with the speed, lightness and musicality demanded by the Petipa choreography. She retired when she married.

Ursula Moreton   Character dancer,
director and teacher. Born in Southsea in
1903, she studied under Cecchetti and
Zanfretta, and it was the latter teacher who
helped her become an excellent mime.

Moreton made her debut with Karsavina
in 1920, joining the Diaghilev Company in
the same year as soloist. She stayed with
them for two years, when she left to join
Massine's company. In 1926 she joined the
de Valois Academy of Choreographic Art
as teacher, and thus became one of the
original members of today's Royal Ballet.
She helped de Valois with the formation of
the Sadler's Wells Theatre Ballet and
became its assistant director and in 1952
became Director of the Royal Ballet School,
receiving the OBE upon her retirement in
1968. She died in 1973 after forty-two years
(with a short break during the war) with
the Company.

Olga Morosova   Russian dancer, wife of Colonel de Basil, born in Moscow. A ballerina for the de Basil Ballets Russes. During her last season at Covent Garden in 1947 Morosova danced the Firebird.

Avril Navarre   A virtuoso classical dancer and soloist for the Sadler's Wells Ballet at Covent Garden. She was particularly noted for her *fouettés* about which one critic wrote, 'She astounded the audience with the brilliance and speed of her *fouettés* in *Les Patineurs'* and, according to whom, her Swanilda in *Coppélia* was 'merry and vivacious'. Even in *Mam'zelle Angot* as a reveller with a violin Massine gave her a show of her *fouettés*!

Vera Nemchinova   Last of Diaghilev's great ballerinas of the twenties, and the first of his new ones to dance Aurora in the memorable but ill-fated production of *The Sleeping Princess* at the Alhambra in 1921.

Nemchinova was born in Moscow in 1899 and was trained by Nelidova, a former Bolshoi ballerina. In 1915 she joined the Diaghilev Ballet as a soloist, and a year later had her first big role as the Can-Can Dancer in Massine's *La Boutique Fantasque*. In 1924 Nemchinova became the Company's leading ballerina, creating the role of the 'page boy' in La Nijinska's *Les Biches*, also in *Les Tentations de la Bergère* and Massine's *Les Matelots*.

In 1927 Nemchinova founded the Nemchinova Dolin Company. In 1930 she became the prima ballerina of the Kaunas Opera Ballet, and in 1936 was with the René Blum Company at the Alhambra as prima ballerina, dancing *Le Lac des Cygnes* and creating the leading role in Fokine's enchanting Chinoiserie ballet *L'Épreuve d'Amour*.

Nemchinova's technical prowess was her greatest asset, and she was famous for her *fouettés*. She retired to open a studio of ballet in New York.

Nadia Nerina (left)   A ballerina with super qualities of lightness, gaiety and a dazzling technique.

Nadia Nerina was born in Cape Town in 1927 where she was trained, and toured the Union until 1945 when she came to England joining the Sadler's Wells Theatre Ballet in 1946 as soloist, becoming a leading ballerina of the Sadler's Wells Ballet (the parent company) at Covent Garden.

Nerina was a sheer joy to watch whether in *Le Lac des Cygnes*, *Giselle*, *The Sleeping Beauty*, *The Firebird*, *Cinderella*, and as Lise, the role she created for Ashton's *La Fille Mal Gardée* in 1960 – perhaps her greatest triumph.

After leaving the company, Nerina twice toured South Africa and Southern Rhodesia with Alexis Rassine as her partner. In 1960 Nerina was the first British ballerina to be guest star at the Bolshoi. She retired in 1966 – a sad loss to many balletomanes.

Claude Newman English mime and character dancer, and teacher. He was born in 1903, and died in 1974. He studied under Phyllis Bedells, Astafieva, and joined the Vic-Wells Ballet in 1931. He was their first male dancer and proved to be of immense use in multi-varied roles: the Bouffon solo in *Casse Noisette* one night and Dr Coppelius another, some of his other best roles were Mr Taylor in *The Prospect Before Us*, Drosslemeyer in *Casse Noisette*, The Tailor in *The Rake's Progress* and in *A Wedding Bouquet* as Ernest.

In 1946 Claude Newman became 'Maître de Ballet' for the Sadler's Wells Theatre Ballet and taught at the school until 1952, after which he retired to work for the Royal Academy of Dancing as examiner, and later as director for the Rome Opera Ballet and the Brazilian Ballet Company of Bahia. He retired in 1970.

Bronislava Nijinska Sister of Nijinsky. She was a dancer, choreographer and ballet mistress.

Born in Minsk in 1891, she studied at the Imperial School, St Petersburg, and joined the Diaghilev Ballet as a soloist in 1909.

It was as a choreographer that Nijinska became famous and in consequence was known as 'La' Nijinska.

Nijinska did choreography all over Europe and America. Hardly a company of importance in the century has not had some ballet done or reproduced by her – the Diaghilev Ballet, Ida Rubenstein Ballet, de Basil Ballet, Ballet Theatre, de Cuevas Ballet, and the Colon Theatre, Buenos Aires, for which she was ballet mistress. In 1935 Nijinska choreographed the dances for Reinhardt's *A Midsummer Night's Dream*.

From 1938 she lived and taught in America, where she choreographed the *Brahms Variations* for Ballet Theatre.

She is chiefly remembered for such ballets as *Les Noces*, *Les Biches*, *Le Train Bleu* and the revival of *The Sleeping Beauty* for the de Cuevas Ballet in Paris 1954.

In 1964 and 1966 she revived *Les Biches* and *Les Noces* for the Royal Ballet.

Nijinska's death in 1972 was the end of a chapter in the history of ballet, for she is recognized as the first internationally known woman choreographer of the twentieth century.

129

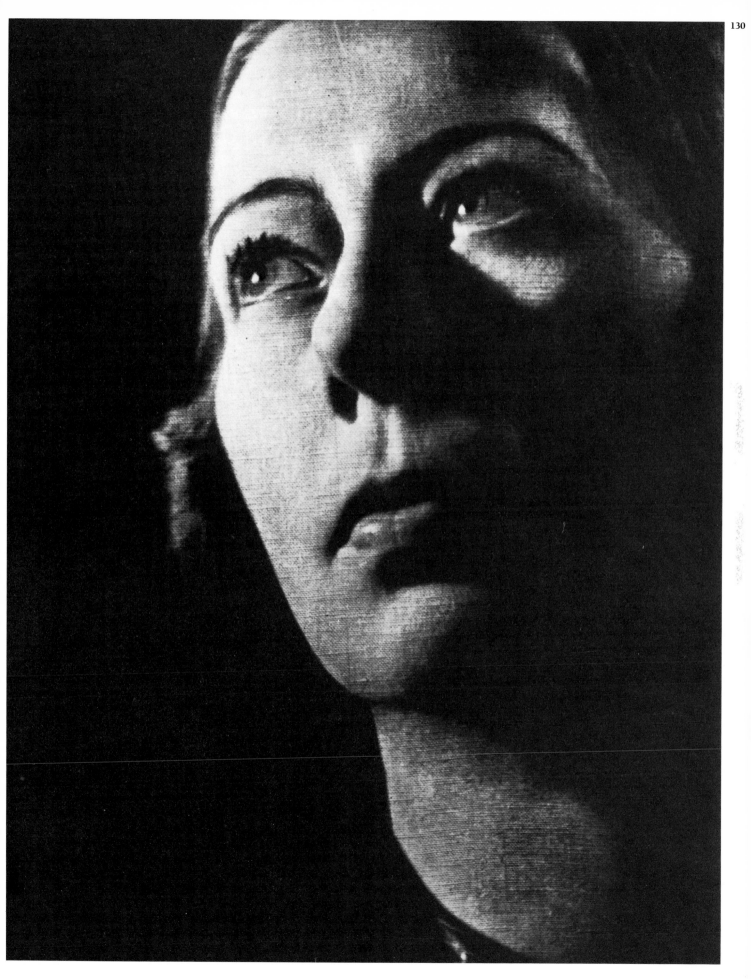

Sono Osato An American dancer born in Omaha of Japanese and American parents. She made her debut in London with de Basil's Ballets Russes, dancing with them from 1934 to 1941. She returned as a principal to dance in America for Ballet Theatre from 1944 to 1945, her most important creation being that of a Lover in Experience in Antony Tudor's classic ballet *Pillar of Fire* in 1942.

After leaving Ballet Theatre, Sono Osato concentrated on musicals such as *On the Town*. She is now retired.

David Paltenghi Danseur noble and
choreographer.

Paltenghi was born in Bournemouth in
1919. He was a pupil of Marie Rambert and
Antony Tudor and made his debut in
1939 with Tudor's London Ballet, joining
the Sadler's Wells Ballet in 1941 and
remaining with them for seven years, after
which he returned to Ballet Rambert as
premier danseur and choreographed the
ballets *Eve of St Agnes, House of Cards,* and
Scherzi Della Sorte, all in 1951.

For Sadler's Wells Ballet Paltenghi created
roles mainly in Robert Helpmann's ballets
such as a Brother in *Comus* and as the King
in *Hamlet.* Later he took over the title role
in this ballet; for Ashton he danced in *The
Quest* and for de Valois in *Promenade.*

As Prince Florimund in *The Sleeping
Beauty* Paltenghi was not only an
exceptionally handsome prince, but an
admirable partner, dancing in the
traditional 'grand manner'. He left ballet to
make films until his death in 1961.

134

Michel Panaieff Premier danseur noble. He was born in Novgorod in 1913, studied with Legat and Egorova, and had his debut in Belgrade. During the thirties Panaieff was premier danseur for the Ballets Russes at Covent Garden and the Alhambra theatres. He created a leading role in Fokine's *Les Elements* at the Alhambra in 1937 but he was principally a classical dancer. He danced *Le Lac des Cygnes* with Danilova both in Monte Carlo and London. During the war Panaieff left for the USA, where he joined Ballet Theatre, which he was with until he retired to teach in Los Angeles.

136

Ailne Phillips Irish ballerina and teacher. Affectionately known to friends and colleagues as 'Babs', she was born in Londonderry in 1905 and trained under Lydia Kyasht, making her debut in musicals. She joined the Carl Rosa Opera Company as première danseuse, after which she joined the Vic-Wells Ballet in 1932 as a principal dancer and assistant teacher to de Valois. She was considered a good technician with a strong precise style, charm and humour of her own. In 1940, after the closing down of the Sadler's Wells Theatre at the beginning of the war, she rejoined the Carl Rosa Opera Company as première danseuse and appeared as guest artist with the International Ballet Company.

In 1946 Babs gave up dancing to concentrate on teaching at the Sadler's Wells Ballet School, becoming its Principal, a post she held from 1946 to 1953. She left to become de Valois's personal assistant, repétiteur to the Company, giving them classes and private lessons at Covent Garden until de Valois sent her to be guest teacher for the Turkish National Ballet and to produce *Coppélia* for them.

Babs retired from 1965 to 1971, owing to the illness of a member of her family. She then returned as guest teacher for the Royal Ballet, taking both company classes and private lessons. I think it fitting here to quote from an article written by Arnold Haskell about her and her work upon the occasion of Margot Fonteyn's return to the Company after an attack of diphtheria in 1953:

'Ailne Phillips is a great teacher, one of the most outstandingly creative teachers of today, working heart and soul for the organization, and being by nature a retiring person she is not known to the public. Miss Phillips is the craftsman behind so many of the dancers we applaud today. It was she who, with both skill and patience restored both Margot Fonteyn and Moira Shearer to the stage after illness, and it is she who is forming the "étoiles" of ten years hence.'

It is true to state that many of the finest ballerinas the Company has produced owe much to Ailne Phillips – Beryl Grey, Svetlana Beriosova, Antoinette Sibley, Nadia Nerina and a host of others.

Marc Platoff   American character dancer
and choreographer. He was born as Marcel
le Platt in Seattle in 1915, and was taught
by Mary Anne Wells and at Cornise South
in Seattle. He joined the de Basil Ballets
Russes as a principal dancer in 1935
remaining with them for four years,
creating and dancing in leading character
roles – Malatesta in Lichine's *Francesca da
Rimini* and King Dodon in Fokine's *Le Coq
d'Or* at Covent Garden in 1937. One can
only describe his performances as
astounding in their dramatic range – the
fierce dances in *Danses Slaves* and *Prince
Igor*, the riotously touching performance as
King Dodon and his monstrously macabre
performance as Malatesta. He then returned
to the USA. As Mark Platt his work in films
and musicals, both dancing and
choreography, is well known in the USA,
and in 1962 he became Director of Ballet at
the Radio City Music Hall.

Peggy van Praagh Dancer, teacher, producer, authoress and director. She was born in London in 1910. Amongst her teachers were Karsavina and Sokolova.

Peggy van Praagh danced for the Camargo Society and with Anton Dolin at the Coliseum. She joined Marie Rambert's Company in 1933, as teacher and principal dancer, for whom she created many roles including those in *Jardin aux Lilas, Dark Elegies, Gala Performance* and *Soirée Musicale* – all Antony Tudor's ballets. She joined him later, becoming a founder member of his London Ballet, for which she was principal dancer and teacher.

In 1941 Peggy van Praagh joined the Sadler's Wells Theatre Ballet as soloist and teacher, eventually becoming its director in 1946. She left to mount ballets for the Royal Ballet on the Continent and in Canada, and in 1960 she became director of the Borovansky Ballet – today's Australian Ballet of which she became director in 1962.

Peggy van Praagh was awarded the OBE and made a Dame of the British Empire for her work with the Royal and Australian ballet companies. She has published three books on ballet.

Alexis Rassine Born of Lithuanian parents. Premier danseur noble, at his best in classical roles – the Bluebird in *The Sleeping Princess (Sleeping Beauty)*, Albrecht in *Giselle*, Prince Florimund in *Sleeping Beauty*, the Prince in *Lac des Cygnes*, all of which he danced with the Sadler's Wells Ballet's seemingly everlasting war-time tours, at the New Theatre and at Covent Garden. He had an excellent technique and impeccable style.

In *Coppélia* Rassine made a most charming and boyish Franz, as the Snob in *Boutique* he caught the wit of the dance equal to that of its creator Idzikovski, and his Elihu in *Job* was danced with immaculate grace and control.

Rassine left the Company to make two successful tours of South Africa and Southern Rhodesia with Nadia Nerina – they made a perfect partnership.

He now runs his own school of ballet in London.

Marie Rambert Born in Warsaw in 1888. Awarded the CBE, in 1954, she was made a Chevalier of the Légion d'Honneur in 1951, and created a Dame of the British Empire in 1962 for her services to British ballet as founder and director of the internationally known Ballet Rambert.

Marie Rambert trained as a dancer, but her real enjoyment and fulfilment of life is as a teacher and impresario. There are many famous dancers, choreographers, designers, and musicians who started life under her encouragement and patronage.

One of the secrets of Rambert's success lies in her almost uncanny flair for spotting talent in the young, and with her good taste, knowledge, drive, vitality and sense of humour she has succeeded in keeping the company and school going for fifty-nine years.

Two excellent books have been published on Dame Marie Rambert – one by Mary Clarke in 1962, *Dancers of Mercury*, and her autobiography in 1972.

Lubov Rostova (right) A soloist of the Ballets Russes who took over roles in *Présages* and *Choreartium* for Massine.

Tatiana Riabouchinska The widow of David Lichine. She was born in Moscow in 1917, trained under Volinine, Kschessinska, and made her debut with the Chauve Souris in Paris in 1932. She joined the de Basil company and remained with them for nine years. Her popularity as one of the 'baby ballerinas' was deservedly immense; her lightness, speed and elevation would have made a UFO jealous! giving many of us our first taste of the Russian school of ballet.

During Riabouchinska's visits with the de Basil company to London she created and danced many leading roles in the repertoire. Those most popular were in *Paganini* by Fokine, *Le Beau Danube*, *Graduation Ball*, *Cendrillon*, and the Golden Cockerel in *Le Coq d'Or*; both in these and as Frivolity in *Les Présages* her performance was memorable for her dancing qualities already mentioned.

Riabouchinska and Lichine went to the USA, where they added to their reputation as guest artists to various companies until they retired to teach in California.

Mrinalini Sarabhai and **Chatunni Panicker**   These two pure classical dancers from India appeared under the auspices of the Royal Academy of Dancing at their Production Club, followed by a short season at the St Martin's Theatre in 1949.

Mrinalini Sarabhai was born in Madras in 1923 and studied at the Kalakshetra Academy of Dramatic Art, making her debut in Madras in 1939. She then travelled in Europe and South America with her own company.

In 1948 Sarabhai founded and directed the Darpana Academy of Dance, Drama, Music and Puppetry at Ahmedabad; she wrote one novel, *This Alone Is True*.

Chatunni Panicker, Sarabhai's partner from 1945 to 1949, taught in her school, and was an expert in Kathakali dancing.

Solange Schwarz   A virtuoso demi-character étoile. Born in Paris in 1910, Solange Schwarz came from a famous family of French dancers, her father being Jean Schwarz of the Paris Opera and well known as a dancer and teacher.

Solange Schwarz was trained at the Opera Ballet School and became étoile of the Opera Comique for seven years, after which she returned to the Paris Opera Ballet as étoile for five years. She then joined Roland Petit's Les Ballets des Champs Elysées, the Ballet de L'Etoile, and de Cuevas and Lifar's Nouveau Ballet de Monte Carlo, before eventually returning to the Paris Opera ballet where she made her last appearance in her favourite role, Swanilda in *Coppélia*, a role in which she was considered incomparable, after which she returned and taught at the Conservatoire. Her own teachers were Zambelli and Nicola Cuerra.

Coppélia 1933

Casse Noisette 193—

Giselle 1934

The Sleeping Princess 1939

Lac des Cygnes 1934

Uday Shankar Pioneering Indian dancer and choreographer. He was born in Udaipur in 1900. An expert on all branches of Indian dancing, as a young man he choreographed for Pavlova and danced with her in the ballet *Radha Krishna*.

Uday Shankar was the first to bring Indian dance culture to Europeans and toured all over the world with his own company. His own style of dancing and production emerged from his knowledge of pure Indian dancing, and he founded a school of dancing in India in 1938.

Nicholas Serguéeff Born in 1876 in St Petersburg, he studied at the Marinsky, becoming a dancer and finally their régisseur general, thereby having all the original dance notations of the classics.

Serguéeff left Russia in 1918. Diaghilev commissioned him to reproduce *The Sleeping Princess* in 1920 at Monte Carlo which was subsequently presented in London in 1921. In 1932 Ninette de Valois commissioned him from Paris to mount all the classics for the Vic-Wells Ballet – *Coppélia* in 1933, *Casse Noisette, Le Lac des Cygnes* and *Giselle* in 1934 and *The Sleeping Princess (Sleeping Beauty)* in 1939.

During the war years Serguéeff was régisseur general for the International Ballet and, once again, he reproduced the classics. He left the company and went to live in Nice where he died in 1951.

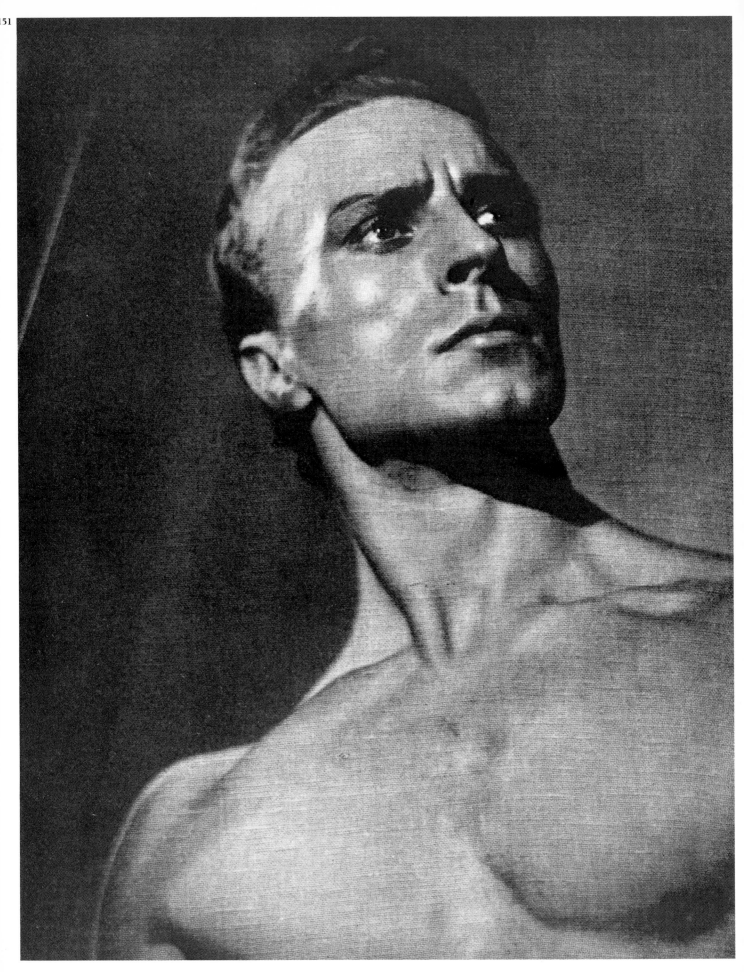

Yurek Shabelevsky A magnificent Polish character dancer. He was born in Warsaw in 1911 and had his early training there. He joined Ida Rubenstein's company in 1928, and the de Basil company in 1932, with which he remained for many years.

Shabelevsky joined the American Ballet Theatre in 1940, after which he became guest artist for ballet companies in South America and Italy. In 1967 he was made ballet master of the New Zealand Ballet Company.

As a dancer Shabelevsky had all the Polish virtuosity and vitality plus a magnetic stage personality and wiry athleticism. He was recognized as the finest character dancer of the period and was immensely popular.

During his visit to Covent Garden with the de Basil Ballet, Shabelevsky danced many roles in *Scheherazade, Jeux d'Enfants, Concurrence* and *Scuola de Ballo*. He excelled as the Polovtsian dancer in *Prince Igor* – his leaping, twistings and *pirouettes en l'air* were classic. To the role of the Golden Slave in *Scheherazade* he brought a fierce 'animal' sensuality. As the puppet in *Petrouchka* he brought out just enough of the 'human' element to make the character macabrely poignant.

154

155

Moira Shearer Scotland's glamorous prima ballerina was born in Dunfermline in 1926. She had her early training in Rhodesia in 1932, coming to England in 1936 for further training with the Fairbairn, Rambert, Legat and Sadler's Wells Schools.

Moira Shearer made her debut with the International Ballet for a year, joining the Sadler's Wells Ballet in 1942, and reached ballerina status in the short space of two years.

Shearer made her Edinburgh debut with the Company, creating the role of a young girl in the park for de Valois's *Promenade*. At her first entrance it was obvious that she not only had beauty and neat and speedy technique but above all 'star' quality, and in no time at all she was a 'name', creating and dancing leading roles in both classical and modern ballets, taking all in her stride.

Shearer left the Company in 1948 to make herself world famous as a film star in the *Red Shoes* in which she danced exquisitely and was perfectly enchanting as an actress, a career she followed and continued after a short return visit as guest artist at Covent Garden. In 1954 she toured America with Robert Helpmann as Titania to his Oberon in *A Midsummer Night's Dream*.

Moira Shearer retired some years ago; she was a shining example and encouragement to future ballerinas for her native Scotland.

Vladimir Skouratoff A premier danseur noble of considerable technical virtuosity, virility and range. He was equally at ease in classical and modern choreography.

Skouratoff was born in Paris in 1925 of Ukrainian parents. He studied under Preobrajenska and Kniaseff, coming to England with Lifar's Nouveau Ballet de Monte Carlo in 1946 as a premier danseur at the Cambridge Theatre where he partnered Renée Jeanmaire. A year later he appeared with the de Basil Ballet at Covent Garden. He was with Roland Petit's Ballets des Champs Elysées and Ballet de Paris from 1948 to 1952 to partner Colette Marchand. Between 1952 and 1970, when he became ballet master of the Bordeaux Ballet, Skouratoff appeared as a guest artist for many companies including the Marquis de Cuevas Ballet, the Scandinavian Ballet Company, the Swedish Ballet Company, the London Festival Ballet, and he spent two years as ballet master for the Strasbourg Ballet.

158

Michael Somes English danseur noble and premier danseur of the Royal Ballet for many years. He was born in Gloucester in 1917, the first student to win a scholarship into the Sadler's Wells Ballet School in 1934 from which he quickly graduated into the Company, becoming premier danseur and well known for his long partnership with Margot Fonteyn with whom he shared his most notable creative successes, all in Frederick Ashton's ballets: in fact Ashton was his mentor and today Somes has charge of all Ashton works for the Royal Ballet. The following ballets are the best-known ones – *Horoscope* (his first creation), *Dante Sonata*, *The Wise Virgins*, *Symphonic Variations*, *Daphnis and Chloë*, *Sylvia*, *Tiresias*, *Ondine*, *Cinderella* and *Birthday Offering*.

Michael Somes was particularly noted for his unusually high elevation. For seven years he was the assistant director of the Company and a principal teacher.

In 1959 Michael Somes was awarded a CBE for his services to the Company and ballet for over twenty years.

Frank Staff   South African dancer, choreographer and director.

Frank Staff was born in Kimberley in 1918, where he was taught by Maude Lloyd and later by Marie Rambert in London. Between 1934 and 1935 he joined the Ballet Rambert and danced with the Sadler's Wells Ballet. He then returned to Ballet Rambert as a principal dancer and choreographer, creating roles in a lot of ballets including *Czerhyana, Peter and the Wolf,* and *Enigma Variations.* Later, he joined the Metropolitan Ballet for which he choreographed *Fanciulla delle Rose.* He also danced for the London Ballet.

In 1938 Frank Staff rejoined the Sadler's Wells Ballet where he created the role of Cupid in Ashton's ballet *Cupid and Psyche,* and in 1940 he created the role of the young peasant boy in Andrée Howard's ballet *La Fête Étrange,* in which he gave a superb performance of subtlety and touching gaucheness. Frank Staff returned to South Africa as director and choreographer for the Cape Town University Ballet Company. He retired from them and joined the Transvaal PACT Ballet Company. In 1970 he became director of the Orange Free State Ballet. He died in 1971.

Nina Tarakanova   An attractive ballerina of great charm and personality, she was born in Moscow in 1915, and trained by Mathilde Kchessinska. She made her debut with Anna Pavlova in 1930. I would describe her as a thistledown dancer, light and frothy, so well suited to the role Massine created for her as the Glove Seller in *Gaîté Parisienne* in 1938 during the René Blum season at the Theatre Royal in Drury Lane, which she re-created for Mona Inglesby's International Ballet Company during the war, when she danced many roles as guest artiste and created the leading role in Mona Inglesby's *Planetomania.*

Tarakanova was a principal dancer for the de Basil Company at Covent Garden, and later the René Blum company at the Theatre Royal, Drury Lane. During this period she had leading roles in ballets such as *Choreartium* and *Seventh Symphony.* She retired to live in London in 1952.

164

Lubov Tchernicheva Born in St Petersburg in 1890 and trained in the Imperial School, she joined the Diaghilev Ballet in 1911 as soloist, to become one of its most popular demi-character dancers, and finally ballet mistress until her retirement in 1929. Tchernicheva was noted, and held in great esteem for, her portrayal of the leading roles in *Thamar*, *Cleopatra* and particularly *Scheherazade*.

Retirement did not suit Tchernicheva so she literally danced out of it in 1935 to appear with de Basil's Ballet as a principal dancer. The three ballets mentioned were revived for her, and a new one specially choreographed for her by David Lichine – *Francesca da Rimini*. She also danced the Miller's Wife in Massine's revival of *Tricorne*.

Tchernicheva retired for the second time and later with her husband Serge Grigorieff remounted *The Firebird*, *Les Sylphides* and *Petrouchka* for the Royal Ballet.

Tchernicheva also took classes.

Both Tchernicheva and her husband died a few years ago – thus sadly one more link with the past has been severed.

165

Nini Theilade (left) Danish dancer and choreographer.

Nini Theilade was trained in Denmark in 1926 as a dancer, but later concentrated mostly on choreography. She created several ballets for the Royal Danish Company.

Nini Theilade made her English debut with the Ballet Russe de Monte Carlo (known as the René Blum company) at Drury Lane in 1938. She made a deep impression not only by her looks but particularly as a character dancer of musical and dramatic qualities. A principal dancer with the company, she made a great success with Leonide Massine, creating the leading role in his ballet of *Nobilissima Visione* and in his *The Seventh Symphony*. She also created the leading role in Fokine's *Les Elements* at the Coliseum in 1937.

Nini Theilade returned to Denmark, receiving the Order of Dannebrog for her work with the ballet.

Tamara Toumanova Film star and one of the greatest classical ballerinas of the century with fabulous looks and personality. She was born near Shanghai in 1919 of Russian parents, studied under Preobrajenska and Balanchine, making an amazing debut at the Paris Opera aged nine in *Le Eventail de Jeanne*. Toumanova joined Balanchine's Les Ballets 1933 and the Ballet Russe de Monte Carlo in 1934 as a ballerina where Balanchine choreographed *La Concurrence* and *Le Cotillon* for her, in which she completely shattered her audiences with the brilliance of her technique and great beauty.

Toumanova was one of three baby ballerinas who made their debut with the de Basil Ballet Russe at the Alhambra in 1933.

Toumanova left the ballet in 1939 to dance in a musical *Stars in Your Eyes*, but returned for a short period and was then off to Hollywood to star in *Days of Glory*, but she left film to become guest artist for the Ballet Theatre, Paris Opera Ballet, the San Francisco Ballet, La Scala, de Cuevas Company and the Festival Ballet in 1952.

Antony Tudor English dancer and choreographer of international fame, noted for his ballets of psychological human relationships. Amongst the most famous are: *Dim Lustre, Undertow, Jardin aux Lilas* and *Pillar of Fire*, of which the latter is considered his masterpiece.

Tudor was born in London in 1909, becoming a pupil of Marie Rambert and Margaret Craske. It was Marie Rambert who gave him his first chance as a choreographer when he choreographed his first ballet *Cross-Garter'd* in 1931. He joined the Vic-Wells Ballet in 1932 as a soloist but, realizing that his *forte* was choreography, he returned to Marie Rambert for whom he created many more ballets.

Tudor left Rambert in 1938 to form his own London Ballet, for which he choreographed *Soirée Musicale* and *Gala Performance*. He left for America in 1939 to join the Ballet Theatre as choreographer and artistic director, for which he created *Pillar of Fire, Romeo and Juliet* among others. He mounted ballets for the New York Metropolitan Opera Ballet Company. In 1962 he became artistic director for the Royal Swedish Ballet and choreographed *Echoing of Trumpets* for them. Later he became a director of the Met. Opera Ballet and worked for other companies.

He choreographed two ballets for the Royal Ballet and one for the Australian Ballet in 1969 and became associate director of the American Ballet Theatre. His influence on American ballet has been of outstanding importance.

Harold Turner Small in stature but great in terpsichorian qualities, Turner was born in Manchester in 1909 to become the first great English demi-character dancer of this century. He was known for such roles as Harlequin in *Carnaval*, the *Bluebird*, the Blueboy in *Les Patineurs* (a role he created in 1937), the Can-Can Dancer in *Boutique Fantasque*, and the Miller in *Le Tricorne*. His work was both virile and vital with a positive animal zest to every role he undertook – the romantic ballets were not suited to him.

Turner danced in musicals and was a principal male dancer for Marie Rambert, the Vic-Wells Ballet and Mona Inglesby's war-time International Ballet. However, his main work was with the Royal Ballet, from which he retired in 1955 to teach at the School. He was ballet master for the Opera ballets until he died tragically of a heart attack whilst rehearsing for the revival of *The Good-Humoured Ladies* in 1962.

175

Ernst Uthoff   Principal dancer, ballet master and founder director of the Chilean National Ballet in 1942. Uthoff was born in Duisburg in Germany in 1904, studied in the Von Laban Central European School of Dance and Drama under Kurt Jooss and Sigurd Leeder, and joined the Ballets Jooss as a principal dancer and assistant ballet master. He danced and created many roles for the company. His best-remembered ones were in *The Green Table*, *The Big City* and in *The Prodigal Son*.

In 1942 Uthoff left the company and founded the Chilean National Ballet in Santiago, from which he retired in 1966 to open a school of ballet in Santiago.

176

Nina Verchinina A Russian dancer born in Moscow, she studied ballet with Preobrajenska, Nijinska and the Central European School of Von Laban. The influence of the latter teacher was paramount in all her work, and dance drama became the basis of all her choreographic works, suiting the individuality of her style and personality.

Verchinina made her debut with Ida Rubenstein in 1929 and joined the de Basil Ballets Russes de Monte Carlo in 1932. Massine created roles for her in *Les Présages, Choreartium*, and *Symphonie Fantastique*, in which he used the Laban system as a basis in his choreography for her.

Verchinina left to work for a year in San Francisco, returning to the Ballets Russes for a further two years. She then left to work in Brazil, where she toured with her own group of dancers, and now has her own school in Copacabana.

Alexander von Swaine A dance recitalist of superhuman vitality and dramatic qualities, he was born in Munich in 1905 and trained by Eugenia Edouardova and Margaret Craske.

Von Swaine danced in Reinhardt's *A Midsummer Night's Dream*, became soloist at La Scala, Milan, and in 1947 did a world tour with his partner Lisa Czobel.

In 1947 he gave a recital at the Arts Theatre in London, and was described as 'a summit in the history of movement' – a 'fiery soul of the dance' – 'possessed by the passion of genuine art'.

183

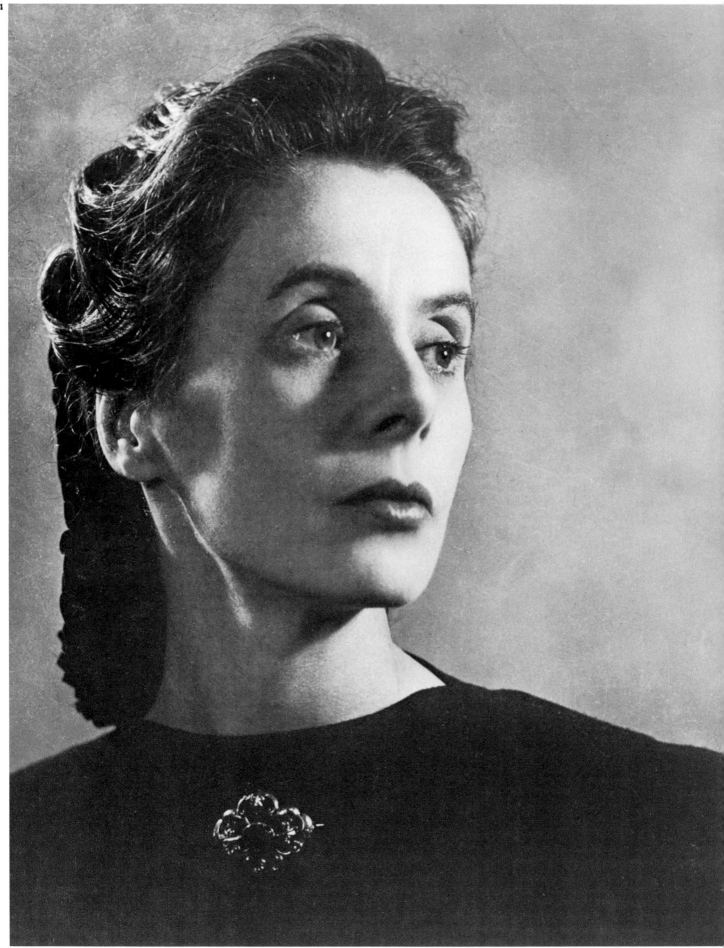

Ninette de Valois   Irish, born at Blessington, Co. Wicklow, Eire on 6 June 1898. A 'practical idealist'. Ballerina, choreographer, authoress, lecturer, teacher and founder of the Royal Ballet and Ballet School (1926), also founder of the Turkish National Ballet.

As a dancer de Valois had charm, elegance, speed and wit – her innate sense of humour has saved many a tricky situation! Trained by Espinosa and Cecchetti, she was première danseuse for the Lyceum Pantomimes from 1914 to 1918. Twice she was prima ballerina for the Italian Opera seasons at Covent Garden, 1918 and 1920. A soloist for Diaghilev (1923–5), she was prima ballerina of the Royal Ballet in its infancy as the Vic-Wells Ballet with guest artists Lydia Lopokova, Markova, Ruth French and Phyllis Bedells. Previous to this she had obtained choreographic exposure at the Festival Theatre, Cambridge, and the Abbey Theatre, Dublin.

Three of de Valois's choreographic works are still in the repertoire of the Royal Ballet and other companies – *Job* (1931), *Checkmate* (1937) and *The Rake's Progress* (1935). She also has three books to her credit – *Invitation to the Ballet* (1937), *Come Dance with Me* (1957) and *Step by Step* (1977).

For services to British ballet de Valois has been awarded the CBE (1947) and was created a Dame of the British Empire in 1951. She is also a Chevalier de la Légion d'Honneur. In 1974 de Valois and Bejart were jointly awarded the Erasmus prize, she for her contribution to classical ballet and he for his to modern works.

Although Dame Ninette retired from the Directorship of the Royal Ballet in 1963 she still retains connections with the Company and with two others, continuing her lecturing and teaching tours, and reproducing her ballets. Her latest work for the Royal Ballet was the production of *The Sleeping Beauty* in 1977.

Igor Youskevitch Was born in Moscow in 1912 and is now a citizen of America. He became a University student when he won many athletic events at Sokol. He took up ballet and in 1932 partnered Zenia Grunt, the Yugoslav prima ballerina. He went to Paris to study under Preobrajinska and joined La Nijinska's Ballets de Paris in 1934. He joined Léon Woizikovski's Ballet in 1935 and toured Australia with de Basil's second company in 1936–37 as a premier danseur. He danced with Ballet Russe de Monte Carlo from 1938–44. In 1944 he joined the U.S. Navy during the War. In 1946 he became guest artist for Massine's Ballet Russe Highlights in America and premier danseur for Ballet Theatre. In 1948 Youskevitch became the premier danseur for Ballet Alicia Alonso. As Harlequin in *Carnaval* with the Russian Company in London he gave a superb performance of virility, agility and whimsicality.

Hans Züllig Dancer and choreographer, teacher and director.

Hans Züllig was born in Rorschach in Switzerland in 1914 and had his training at Essen and Dartington Hall with Jooss; he became a principal dancer of the Ballets Jooss. In 1954 Züllig succeeded Jooss as Principal of the Folkwang Schule at Essen.

In 1947 Züllig left the company to work in films and musicals; then, in 1949, he joined the Sadler's Wells Theatre Ballet as soloist, leaving them in the same year to rejoin the Ballets Jooss in Essen, and from 1956 for five years taught in Chile. He choreographed *Le Bosquet* in 1945.

A smallish man with great charm and wiry, airborne athleticism – romance and drama were his other chief assets. He created leading roles in *Chronica, The Big City, A Spring Tale, A Ball in Old Vienna, The Seven Heroes* and others.

APPENDICES

Appendix 1

We have, to the best of our ability, been accurate on the details of which company dancers were appearing with when these photographs were taken (this is the date shown). The names given are as they were then; Ballet Theatre is now American Ballet Theatre and Festival Ballet is London Festival Ballet. The tangled knot of the various Ballets Russes has been dealt with, as far as possible, with the help of Kathrine Sorley Walker whose forthcoming book on the subject is eagerly awaited.

1   Igor Yousskevitch, composite study from *Carnaval*. Ballet Russe de Monte Carlo, 1938. Choreography : Michael Fokine

2   Margot Fonteyn in the polka from *Façade*. Vic-Wells Ballet, Sadler's Wells Theatre, London 1935. Choreography : Frederick Ashton

3   Youly Algaroff as Albrecht in *Giselle*. Lifar's Nouveau Ballet de Monte Carlo, Cambridge Theatre, London 1946. Choreography : Jean Coralli and Jules Perrot

4   Algeranoff as the Astrologer in *Le Coq d'Or*. de Basil's Ballets Russes, Royal Opera House, Covent Garden, 1937. Choreography : Michael Fokine

5   Alicia Alonso. Portrait, 1946

6   Alicia Alonso as Kitri in *Don Quixote*. Ballet Theatre, Royal Opera House, 1946. Choreography : after Petipa

7   Antonio in *Zapateado*. Cambridge Theatre, London 1951

8   Pearl Argyle in *Le Roi Nu*. Vic-Wells Ballet, Sadler's Wells Theatre, London 1938. Choreography : Ninette de Valois

9   Pearl Argyle as Venus in *The Judgement of Paris*. Vic-Wells Ballet, Sadler's Wells Theatre, London 1938. Choreography : Frederick Ashton

10   Frederick Ashton as the Hussar in *Apparitions*. Vic-Wells Ballet, Sadler's Wells Theatre, 1936. Choreography : Frederick Ashton

11   Irina Baronova as The Queen of Shemakhan in *Le Coq d'Or*. de Basil's Ballets Russes, Royal Opera House, Covent Garden, 1937. Choreography : Michael Fokine

12   Irina Baronova as Passion in *Les Présages*. Ballets Russes de Monte Carlo, Alhambra Theatre, London 1933. Choreography : Leonide Massine

13 and 14   Svetlana Beriosova as the Sugar Plum Fairy in *Casse Noisette*. Sadler's Wells Theatre Ballet, Sadler's Wells Theatre, London 1950. Choreography : after Petipa

15   David Blair. Portrait, 1947

16   David Blair as Captain Belaye in *Pineapple Poll*. Sadler's Wells Theatre Ballet, Sadler's Wells Theatre, 1951. Choreography : John Cranko

17   Edouard Borovansky as the Artist in *Le Lion Amoureux*. de Basil's Ballets Russes, Royal Opera House, Covent Garden, 1937. Choreography : David Lichine

18   Patricia Bowman in a study called 'The Water Nymph'. 1937

19   Oleg Briansky. Portrait, 1952

20   Oleg Briansky in the solo from *Don Quixote*. Festival Ballet, Royal Festival Hall, London 1952. Choreography : after Petipa

21   Janine Charrat as the Princess Daredjan in *Chota Roustaveli*. Lifar's Nouveau Ballet de Monte Carlo, Cambridge Theatre, London 1946. Choreography : Serge Lifar

22   Janine Charrat in *Priére*. Lifar's Nouveau Ballet de Monte Carlo, Cambridge Theatre, London 1946. Choreography : Serge Lifar

23   Alan Carter as the Harlequin in *Harlequin in the Street*. Vic-Wells Ballet, Sadler's Wells Theatre, London 1938. Choreography : Frederick Ashton

24   William Chappell as a skater in *Les Patineurs*. Vic-Wells Ballet, Sadler's Wells Theatre, London 1937. Choreography : Frederick Ashton

25   Yvette Chauviré as the Princess Daredjan in *Chota Roustaveli*. Lifar's Nouveau Ballet de Monte Carlo, Cambridge Theatre, London 1946. Choreography : Serge Lifar

26   Pauline Clayden as the Suicide in *Miracle in the Gorbals*. Sadler's Wells Ballet, Princes Theatre, London 1944. Choreography : Robert Helpmann

27   Margaret Dale as the Princess Florine in *The Sleeping Beauty*. Sadler's Wells Ballet, Royal Opera House, Covent Garden, 1946. Choreography : after Petipa

28   Margaret Dale as the Sugar Plum Fairy in *Casse Noisette*. Sadler's Wells Ballet, New Theatre, London 1944. Choreography : after Petipa

29   Alexandra Danilova in the title role of *The Firebird*. de Basil's Ballets Russes, Royal Opera House, Covent Garden, 1936. Choreography : Michael Fokine

30   Alexandra Danilova as the Serving Maid in *The Gods Go A'Begging*. de Basil's Ballets Russes, Royal Opera House, Covent Garden, 1936. Choreography : David Lichine

31   Alexandra Danilova and Roman Jasinsky in *Francesca da Rimini*. de Basil's Ballets Russes, Royal Opera House, Covent Garden, 1937. Choreography : David Lichine

32   Anton Dolin as the Tzarevitch in *The Firebird*. Covent Garden, 1938. Choreography : Michael Fokine

33   Anton Dolin as Satan in *Job*. Sadler's Wells Ballet, Royal Opera House, Covent Garden, 1948. Choreography : Ninette de Valois

34   Anton Dolin as *David* in the ballet of the same name. Markova-Dolin Ballet, Theatre Royal Newcastle-upon-Tyne, 1935. Choreography : Keith Lester

35   Leslie Edwards as the Beggar in *Miracle in the Gorbals*. Sadler's Wells Ballet, Princes Theatre,

London 1944. Choreography : Robert Helpmann

36   Leslie Edwards as Bilby in *A Mirror for Witches*. Sadler's Wells Ballet, Royal Opera House, Covent Garden, 1952. Choreography : Andrée Howard

37 and 38   André Eglevsky as Paris in *Helen of Troy*. Ballet Theatre, Royal Opera House, Covent Garden, 1946. Choreography : David Lichine

39   Richard Ellis as the Officer in *Mam'zelle Angot*. Sadler's Wells Ballet, Royal Opera House, Covent Garden, 1947. Choreography : Leonide Massine

40   Julia Farron as Psyche in *Cupid and Psyche*. Vic-Wells Ballet, Sadler's Wells Theatre, London 1939. Choreography : Frederick Ashton

41   Julia Farron as The Red Queen in *Checkmate*. Sadler's Wells Ballet, Royal Opera House, Covent Garden, 1948. Choreography : Ninette de Valois

42   Violetta Elvin as the Princess Florine in *The Sleeping Beauty*. Sadler's Wells Ballet, Royal Opera House, Covent Garden, 1946. Choreography : after Petipa

43   Violetta Elvin. Portrait, 1946

44   Violetta Elvin in the title role of *Giselle*. Sadler's Wells Ballet, Royal Opera House, Covent Garden, 1946. Choreography : Jean Coralli and Jules Perrot.

45   John Field in the title role of *Tiresias*. Sadler's Wells Ballet, Royal Opera House, Covent Garden, 1951. Choreography : Frederick Ashton

46   Elaine Fifield in the title role of *Pineapple Poll*. Sadler's Wells Theatre Ballet, Sadler's Wells Theatre, 1951. Choreography : John Cranko

47   Michael Fokine. Portrait, 1938

48   Frederic Franklin in *The Seventh Symphony*. Ballet Russe de Monte Carlo, Theatre Royal, Drury Lane, 1938. Choreography : Leonide Massine

49   Margot Fonteyn as the Princess Aurora in *The Sleeping Princess*. Vic-Wells Ballet, Sadler's Wells Theatre, London 1939. Choreography : after Petipa

50   Margot Fonteyn in the title role of *Giselle*. Vic-Wells Ballet, Sadler's Wells Theatre, London 1937. Choreography : Jean Coralli and Jules Perrot

51   Margot Fonteyn as the Princess Aurora in *The Sleeping Princess*. Vic-Wells Ballet, Sadler's Wells Theatre, London 1939. Choreography : after Petipa

52   Margot Fonteyn in *Pomona*. Vic-Wells Ballet, Sadler's Wells Theatre, London 1937. Choreography : Frederick Ashton

53   Margot Fonteyn in *Nocturne*. Vic-Wells Ballet, Sadler's Wells Theatre, London 1937. Choreography : Frederick Ashton

54   Margot Fonteyn in the title role of *Giselle*. Sadler's Wells Ballet, Royal Opera House, Covent Garden, 1946. Choreography : Jean Coralli and Jules Perrot

55   Margot Fonteyn as Venus in *The Judgement of*

Paris. Vic-Wells Ballet, Sadler's Wells Theatre, London 1938. Choreography: Frederick Ashton

56 Margot Fonteyn in *Apparitions*. Vic-Wells Ballet, Sadler's Wells Theatre, London 1937. Choreography: Frederick Ashton

57 Margot Fonteyn and Alexis Rassine in *Le Spectre de la Rose*. Sadler's Wells Ballet, New Theatre, London 1944. Choreography: Michael Fokine

58 Margot Fonteyn and Frederick Ashton in *Nocturne*. Vic-Wells Ballet, Sadler's Wells Theatre, London 1936. Choreography: Frederick Ashton

59 Margot Fonteyn and Michael Somes in *Dante Sonata*. Sadler's Wells Ballet, Sadler's Wells Theatre, London 1937. Choreography: Frederick Ashton

60 Margot Fonteyn and Robert Helpmann in *Les Patineurs*. Vic-Wells Ballet, Sadler's Wells Theatre, London 1937. Choreography: Frederick Ashton

61 Celia Franca as the Queen of the Wilis in *Giselle*. Sadler's Wells Ballet, New Theatre, London 1941. Choreography: Jean Coralli and Jules Perrot

62 Sally Gilmour as Mrs Tebrick in *Lady into Fox*. Ballet Rambert, Mercury Theatre, London 1936. Choreography: Andrée Howard

63 John Gilpin. Portrait, 1952

64 John Gilpin in *The Vision of Marguerite*. Festival Ballet, Royal Festival Hall, London 1952. Choreography: Frederick Ashton

65 Nana Gollner as Odette in *Le Lac des Cygnes*. International Ballet, Gaumont Theatre, Kilburn, London 1947. Choreography: after Petipa/Ivanov

66 Nana Gollner and Paul Petroff as Swanilda and Franz in *Coppelia*. International Ballet, Gaumont Theatre, Kilburn, London 1947. Choreography: Serguéeff after Petipa

67 Ram Gopal, Saville Theatre, London 1948

68 Alexander Grant and Pauline Clayden in *Les Sirènes*. Sadler's Wells Ballet, Royal Opera House, Covent Garden, 1946. Choreography: Frederick Ashton

69 Tamara Grigorieva in *The Good Humoured Ladies*. de Basil's Ballets Russes, Royal Opera House, Covent Garden, London 1935. Choreography: Leonide Massine

70 Tamara Grigorieva as Francesca in *Francesca da Rimini*. da Basil's Ballets Russes, Royal Opera House, Covent Garden, London 1937. Choreography: David Lichine

71 Beryl Grey as Odette in *Le Lac des Cygnes*. Sadler's Wells Ballet, Royal Opera House, Covent Garden, 1946. Choreography: after Petipa/Ivanov

72 Beryl Grey in the title role of *Giselle*. Sadler's Wells Ballet, Royal Opera House, Covent Garden, 1946. Choreography: Jean Coralli and Jules Perrot

73 Beryl Grey as the Lilac Fairy in *The Sleeping Beauty*. Sadler's Wells Ballet, Royal Opera House, Covent Garden, 1946. Choreography: after Petipa

74 Beryl Grey as the Princess Aurora in *The Sleeping Beauty*. Sadler's Wells Ballet, Royal Opera House, Covent Garden, 1946. Choreography: after Petipa

75 Gordon Hamilton as Mr Taylor in *The Prospect Before Us*. Sadler's Wells Ballet, New Theatre, London 1943. Choreography: Ninette de Valois

76 Gordon Hamilton as Bouffon in *Casse Noisette*. Sadler's Wells Ballet, New Theatre, London 1942. Choreography: after Petipa

77 Gordon Hamilton as Madge in *La Sylphide*. Ballets des Champs Elysées, Winter Garden Theatre, London 1947. Choreography: Victor Gsovsky

78 John Hart as Prince Florimund in *The Sleeping Beauty*. Sadler's Wells Ballet, Royal Opera House, Covent Garden, 1947. Choreography: after Petipa

79 John Hart as the Corregidor in *Le Tricorne*. Sadler's Wells Ballet, Royal Opera House, Covent Garden, 1947. Choreography: Leonide Massine

80 Robert Helpmann as Carabosse in *The Sleeping Beauty*. Sadler's Wells Ballet, Royal Opera House, Covent Garden, 1946. Choreography: after Petipa

81 Robert Helpmann in the title role of *Hamlet*. Sadler's Wells Ballet, New Theatre, London 1942. Choreography: Robert Helpmann

82 Robert Helpmann in the title role of *Prometheus*. Vic-Wells Ballet, Sadler's Wells Theatre, London 1936. Choreography: Ninette de Valois

83 Pearl Argyle and Robert Helpmann in *Pomona*. Vic-Wells Ballet, Sadler's Wells Theatre, London 1933. Choreography: Frederick Ashton

84 Mary Honer and Robert Helpmann in *A Wedding Bouquet*. Vic-Wells Ballet, Sadler's Wells Theatre, London 1937. Choreography: Frederick Ashton

85 Mary Honer as the Sugar Plum Fairy in *Casse Noisette*. Vic-Wells Ballet, Sadler's Wells Theatre, London 1937. Choreography: after Petipa

86 Mary Honer and Harold Turner as the Bluebirds in *The Sleeping Princess*. Vic-Wells Ballet, Sadler's Wells Theatre, London 1939. Choreography: after Petipa

87 Mona Inglesby as the Bride in *Amoras*. International Ballet, Cambridge Theatre, London 1941. Choreography: Mona Inglesby

88 Mona Inglesby in *Endymion*. International Ballet, Cambridge Theatre, London 1941. Choreography: Mona Inglesby

89 Renée Jeanmarie in *Piccoli*. Original Ballet Russe, Royal Opera House, Covent Garden, 1947. Choreography: Boris Kniaseff

90 Renée Jeanmaire as the Princess Aurora in *Aurora's Wedding*. Original Ballet Russe, Royal Opera House, Covent Garden, 1947. Choreography: after Petipa

91 Kurt Jooss in *Chronica*. Ballets Jooss, Old Vic Theatre, London 1939. Choreography: Kurt Jooss

92 and 93 Alexandre Kalionjny as the Golden Slave in *Scheherazade*. Nouveau Ballet de Monte Carlo, Cambridge Theatre, London 1946. Choreography: Michael Fokine

94 Nora Kaye as Juliet in *Romeo and Juliet*. Ballet Theatre, Royal Opera House, Covent Garden, 1946. Choreography: Antony Tudor

95 Nora Kaye in *La Gloire*. New York City Ballet, Royal Opera House, Covent Garden, 1952. Choreography: Antony Tudor

96 Michael Kidd in the title role of *Petrouchka*. Ballet Theatre, Royal Opera House, Covent Garden, 1946. Choreography: Michael Fokine

97 Michael Kidd as the Handyman in *On Stage*. Ballet Theatre, Royal Opera House, Covent Garden, 1946. Choreography: Michael Kidd

98 John Kriza in *Interplay*. Ballet Theatre, Royal Opera House, Covent Garden, 1946. Choreography: Jerome Robbins

99 and 100 Hugh Laing as Romeo in *Romeo and Juliet*. Ballet Theatre, Royal Opera House, Covent Garden, 1946. Choreography: Antony Tudor

101 Gerd Larsen as the Fairy of the Crystal Fountain in the prologue of *The Sleeping Beauty*. Sadler's Wells Ballet, Royal Opera House, Covent Garden, 1946. Choreography: after Petipa

102 Yura Lazowski as a Polovtsian Warrior in *Prince Igor*. de Basil's Ballets Russes, Royal Opera House, Covent Garden, 1937. Choreography: Michael Fokine

103 Yura Lazowski as the Jailor in *Symphonie Fantastique*. de Basil's Ballets Russes, Royal Opera House, Covent Garden, 1937. Choreography: Leonide Massine

104 Henry Legerton as the Shop Assistant in *La Boutique Fantasque*. Sadler's Wells Ballet, Royal Opera House, Covent Garden, 1947. Choreography: Leonide Massine

105 Henry Legerton as The Rake in *The Rake's Progress*. Sadler's Wells Ballet, Royal Opera House, Covent Garden, 1947. Choreography: Ninette de Valois

106 Serge Lifar in *Icare*, Nouveau Ballet de Monte Carlo, Cambridge Theatre, London 1946. Choreography: Serge Lifar

107 Catherine Littlefield in *Terminal*. The Philadelphia Ballet Company, Hippodrome Theatre, London 1937. Choreography: Catherine Littlefield

108 and 109 Dorothie Littlefield in *Barn Dance*. The Philadelphia Ballet Company, Hippodrome Theatre, London 1937. Choreography: Catherine Littlefield

110 Alicia Markova as Odile in *Le Lac des Cygnes*. Vic-Wells Ballet, Sadler's Wells Theatre, London 1934. Choreography: after Petipa

111 Alicia Markova as the Muse in *The Beloved One*. Markova-Dolin Company, Kings Theatre, Hammersmith, London 1937. Choreography: Bronislava Nijinska

112 Alicia Markova. Study, 1938.

113 Alicia Markova in the adagietto from *The House Party (Les Biches)*. Markova-Dolin Ballet, Kings Theatre, Hammersmith, London 1937. Choreography: Bronislava Nijinska

114 Leonide Massine as the Miller in *Le Tricorne*. de Basil's Ballets Russes, Royal Opera House, Covent Garden, 1936. Choreography: Leonide Massine

115 Leonide Massine in *Jardin Public*. de Basil's Ballets Russes, Royal Opera House, Covent Garden, 1936. Choreography: Leonide Massine

116 and 117 Tamara Toumanova and Leonide Massine in *Symphonie Fantastique*. de Basil's Ballets Russes, Royal Opera House, Covent Garden, 1937. Choreography: Leonide Massine

118 Pamela May as the Fairy in *Baiser de la Fee*. Vic-Wells Ballet, Sadler's Wells Theatre, London 1935. Choreography: Frederick Ashton

119 Pamela May as the Rose Fairy in the prologue of *The Sleeping Princess*. Vic-Wells Ballet, Sadler's Wells Theatre, London 1939. Choreography: after Petipa

120 Pamela May as the Princess Aurora in *The Sleeping Beauty*. Sadler's Wells Ballet, Royal Opera House, Covent Garden, 1946. Choreography: after Petipa

121 Pamela May and Harold Turner in *La Boutique Fantasque*. Sadler's Wells Ballet, Royal Opera House, Covent Garden, 1947. Choreography: Leonide Massine

122 Elizabeth Miller as the Fairy of the Song

Birds in the prologue of *The Sleeping Princess*. Vic-Wells Ballet, Sadler's Wells Theatre, London 1939. Choreography: after Petipa

123   Ursula Moreton as the Dancer in *The Rake's Progress*. Vic-Wells Ballet, Sadler's Wells Theatre, London 1935. Choreography: Ninette de Valois

124   Olga Morosova in *Le Coq d'Or*. de Basil's Ballets Russes, Royal Opera House, Covent Garden, 1937. Choreography: Michael Fokine

125   Avril Navarre in *Les Patineurs*. Sadler's Wells Ballet, Royal Opera House, Covent Garden, 1947. Choreography: Frederick Ashton

126   Vera Nemchinova in *L'Epreuve d'Amour*. René Blum's Ballets de Monte Carlo, Alhambra Theatre, London 1936. Choreography: Michael Fokine

127   Nadia Nerina in *Les Sylphides*. Sadler's Wells Ballet, Sadler's Wells Theatre, London 1946. Choreography: Michael Fokine

128   Nadia Nerina in the title role of *Cinderella*. Sadler's Wells Ballet, Royal Opera House, Covent Garden, 1949. Choreography: Frederick Ashton

129   Claude Newman in a composite picture as the Tailor in *The Rake's Progress* and Herr Drosselmeyer in *Casse Noisette*. Vic-Wells Ballet, Sadler's Wells Theatre, 1934 and 1935. Choreography: Ninette de Valois and after Petipa

130   La Nijinska. Portrait, 1936.

131   Sono Osato in *Le Coq d'Or*. de Basil's Ballets Russes, Royal Opera House, Covent Garden, 1937. Choreography: Michael Fokine

132   Sono Osato. Portrait, 1937

133   David Paltenghi in the title role of *Hamlet*. Sadler's Wells Ballet, New Theatre, London 1942. Choreography: Robert Helpmann

134   David Paltenghi and Julia Farron in *Miracle in the Gorbals*. Sadler's Wells Ballet, Princes Theatre, London 1944. Choreography: Robert Helpmann

135   Michel Panaieff. Study, 1937

136   Ailne Phillips. Portrait, 1937

137   Ailne Phillips in *Les Rendezvous*. Vic-Wells Ballet, Sadler's Wells Theatre, London 1937. Choreography: Frederick Ashton

138   Marc Platoff in *Danses Slaves et Danses Tziganes*. de Basil's Ballets Russes, Royal Opera House, Covent Garden, 1937. Choreography: Michael Fokine

139   Marc Platoff as Malatesta in *Francesca da Rimini*. de Basil's Ballets Russes, Royal Opera House, Covent Garden, 1937. Choreography: David Lichine

140 and 141   Peggy van Praagh in *Soirée Musicale*. London Ballet, Arts Theatre, London 1940. Choreography: Antony Tudor

142   Marie Rambert. Portrait, 1948

143   Alexis Rassine as the Bluebird in *The Sleeping Princess*. Sadler's Wells Ballet, New Theatre, London 1942. Choreography: after Petipa

144   Tatiana Riabouchinska as *Le Coq d'Or*. de Basil's Ballets Russes, Royal Opera House, Covent Garden, 1937. Choreography: Michael Fokine

145   Tatiana Riabouchinska. Portrait, 1938

146   Lubov Rostova. Study, 1933

147   Mrinalini Sarabhai and Chatunni Panicker. St Martin's Theatre, London 1949

148   Solange Schwarz in *Les Forains*. Les Ballets des Champs Elysées, Adelphi Theatre, London 1946. Choreography: Roland Petit

149   Nicholas Serguéeff. Study, 1940

150   Uday Shankar and partner, 1935

151   Yurek Shabelevsky. Study, 1933

152   Yurek Shabelevsky as a Polovtsian Warrior in *Prince Igor*. Ballets Russes de Monte Carlo, Alhambra Theatre, London 1933. Choreography: Michael Fokine

153   Yurek Shabelevsky as the Tramp in *La Concurrence*. de Basil's Ballets Russes, Alhambra Theatre, London 1936. Choreography: Georges Balanchine

154 and 155   Moira Shearer as the Princess Aurora in *The Sleeping Beauty*. Sadler's Wells Ballet, Royal Opera House, Covent Garden, 1946. Choreography: after Petipa

156   Vladimir Skouratoff in *Protée*. Nouveau Ballet de Monte Carlo, Cambridge Theatre, London 1951. Choreography: David Lichine

157   Michael Somes. Study, 1947

158   Michael Somes as the Red Knight in *Checkmate*. Sadler's Wells Ballet, Royal Opera House, Covent Garden, 1948. Choreography: Ninette de Valois

159   Michael Somes. Study, 1947

160   Frank Staff as Cupid in *Cupid and Psyche*. Vic-Wells Ballet, Sadler's Wells Theatre, London 1939. Choreography: Frederick Ashton

161 and 162   Nina Tarakanova as the Glove Seller in *Gaité Parisienne*. Ballet Russe de Monte Carlo, Theatre Royal, Drury Lane, London 1938. Choreography: Leonide Massine

163   Nina Tarakanova as The Doll in *Petrouchka*. de Basil's Ballets Russes de Monte Carlo, Royal Opera House, Covent Garden, 1933. Choreography: Michael Fokine

164   Lubov Tchernicheva in the title role of *Thamar*. de Basil's Ballets Russes, Royal Opera House, Covent Garden, 1936. Choreography: Michael Fokine

165   Lubov Tchernicheva as Zobeide in *Scheherazade*. de Basil's Ballets Russes, Royal Opera House, Covent Garden, 1937. Choreography: Michael Fokine

166   Lubov Tchernicheva as Francesca in *Francesca da Rimini*. de Basil's Ballets Russes, Royal Opera House, Covent Garden, 1937. Choreography: David Lichine

167   Nini Theilade in *The Seventh Symphony*. Ballet Russe de Monte Carlo, Theatre Royal, Drury Lane, 1938. Choreography: Leonide Massine

168   Tamara Toumanova in *Aurora's Wedding*. Ballet Russe de Monte Carlo, Theatre Royal, Drury Lane, 1938. Choreography: after Petipa

169   Tamara Toumanova as The Miller's Wife in *Le Tricorne*. Ballet Russe de Monte Carlo, Theatre Royal, Drury Lane, 1938. Choreography: Leonide Massine

170   Tamara Toumanova as the Girl in *Le Spectre de la Rose*. Ballet Russe de Monte Carlo, Royal Opera House, Covent Garden, 1938. Choreography: Michael Fokine

171   Antony Tudor and Elisabeth Schooling in *The Descent of Hebe*. Ballet Rambert, Mercury Theatre, London 1935. Choreography: Antony Tudor

172 and 173   Harold Turner as The Rake in *The Rake's Progress*. Vic-Wells Ballet, Sadler's Wells Theatre, London 1937. Choreography: Ninette de Valois

174   Harold Turner as The Red Knight in *Checkmate*. Vic-Wells Ballet, Sadler's Wells Theatre, London 1937. Choreography: Ninette de Valois.

175–177   Ernst Uthoff in the title role of *The Prodigal Son*. Ballets Jooss, Savoy Theatre, London 1933. Choreography: Kurt Jooss

178   Noelle de Mosa and Ernst Uthoff in *The Big City*. Ballets Jooss, Savoy Theatre, London 1933. Choreography: Kurt Jooss

179   Elsa Kahl and Ernst Uthoff in *The Green Table*. Ballets Jooss, Savoy Theatre, London 1933. Choreography: Kurt Jooss

180 and 181   Nina Verchinina in *Choreartium*. Ballets Russes de Monte Carlo, Alhambra Theatre, London 1933. Choreography: Leonide Massine

182   Nina Verchinina. Portrait, 1933

183   Alexander von Swaine in the *Spanish Dance*. Arts Theatre, London 1947. Choreography: Alexander von Swaine

184   Ninette de Valois. Portrait, 1946

185   Ninette de Valois and Robert Helpmann in *Douanes*. Vic-Wells Ballet, Sadler's Wells Theatre, London 1935. Choreography: Ninette de Valois

186   Igor Youskevitch and Alicia Markova in *The Seventh Symphony*. Ballet Russe de Monte Carlo, Theatre Royal, Drury Lane, 1938. Choreography: Leonide Massine

187   Hans Züllig in *A Spring Tale*. Ballets Jooss, Old Vic Theatre, London 1939. Choreography: Kurt Jooss

188   Hans Züllig and Ulla Soederbaum in *A Spring Tale*. Ballets Jooss, Old Vic Theatre, London 1939. Choreography: Kurt Jooss

Appendix 2
Dancers and the Camera *

The technique of photographing dancers in action in the studio is entirely different from that on the stage, and as I have specialized in the former for fifteen years, I prefer to deal with the subject from that angle.

First of all I should mention that for thirty years I have been a keen follower of the ballet and have studied it twice in my life, once during that time and once as a child. On that account I am extremely sensitive and sympathetic towards the dancers and am very critical of photographs taken of them. I am also fully aware that some of my own are by no means beyond criticism! In fact, I have on many occasions scrapped 'action shots', excellent from my point of view, on account of the apparent awkwardness of the dancer – I say 'apparent' because, although the camera does not lie, ill-advised lighting and camera angle can play havoc with the best of figures.

In such things as the use of suitable backgrounds, etc., studio action photographs vary little from those of the old posed pictures, which I think hardly exist any longer, for even at one-tenth of a second one can get an arabesque or any other static pose, provided the operator knows enough to catch the pose at its peak. This is only attained by experience, as he 'takes' a split second before that point is reached in the same way as rifle-shooting at a moving object.

To imagine that dancers are easy to photograph is one of those beautiful illusions of life, for in fact it is one of the most exacting of jobs, requiring (on both sides) an enormous amount of patience and practice. However, once confidence is attained it becomes comparatively easy.

I take three types of pictures, as follows: First, commercial (Fig. 1), including straight heads and full lengths with little or no background, for daily press and programme work; second, pictorial (Fig. 2) and more complicated pictures, with background or special lighting effects, for the weeklies and periodicals of the better kind, likewise front-of-house pictures and books; and third, the purely decorative type where, although the dancer does not actually predominate, the whole would be incomplete without her (Fig.

*First published 1949.

Fig. 1

3). This latter type is essentially for large-size reproduction, for being full of detail it is wasted in any size smaller than 10 in by 8 in, and in my opinion should never be used for the more popular kind of publicity such as postcards and cheaper reproductions for sale in theatres, but should be kept for books and exhibitions. Commercially, therefore, it is of

Fig. 2

less use, and anyone taking up the ballet as a medium for that sort of work will find that type two will cover them sufficiently.

It is extremely difficult to lay down definite rules for taking pictures – the fatal error of most textbooks – but a number of points to be watched carefully may be of great help and for that reason are tabulated under the following headings: (a) Backgrounds and lighting; (b) Cameras and films; (c) Retouching, etc.

(a) BACKGROUNDS AND LIGHTING

The ideal, in my opinion, is the use of an all-white background, graduating to a medium grey in the immediate foreground (this applies whether the backcloth or wall is of any colour or tone), which gives a sense of space and distance and which is as useful for projecting shadow backgrounds as it is for colour lighting. However, in both these cases the fact that the subject and background should be separately lit means a minimum sized studio of 30 ft long by 15 ft wide and 11 ft high – not easily attainable. So for the amateur and smaller studio, where the light for the subject cannot be cut off from the backcloth, the most suitable would be a medium grey. Although this would tone down the dramatic effect of pictures relying upon shadow work, it has the merit of softening down unavoidable shadows which if strong would spoil the general effect.

Of course, there are many different ways of making backgrounds, which should wherever possible assist the subject either by following his or her 'line' by single lighting, or by bringing out the feeling of the ballet story. Sometimes the mere shadow of another person in the ballet will do this with, I think, reasonable effect.

Then there is the table-top method using a montage where the *décor* is made and photographed separately, and the dancer then photographed using the first negative on the ground glass for 'placing' and composition.

Fig. 3

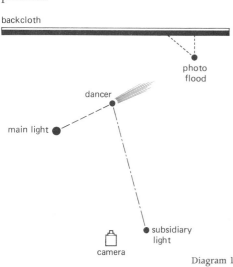

backcloth

photo flood

dancer

main light

subsidiary light

camera

Diagram 1

An excellent picture can be made by the use of a 500-watt floodlight and bowl reflector, with a subsidiary light nearer the camera to prevent a dead black on the unlit side. This could be added to if a portable 500- or photo-floodlight is available by placing it near the background, thus throwing the *unlit* side of the subject into relief and adding both strength and a dramatic sense to the picture, as in Diagram 1.

The spotlight is of immense value for bringing up highlights upon the subject, both for dramatic effect and giving a three-dimensional value. It can also be used with good effect in a similar way to that of the backcloth light mentioned previously, only in this case it outlines the figure in white, the reverse of the silhouette.

Although the most effective of all forms of lighting, the spotlight can also produce some unfortunate results when misused, as occurs only too frequently when it is used as the main form of light. In this case the beam is usually not large enough to cover the dancer entirely, so that her arms and back leg are partly in shadow, giving them the appearance of being amputated. It also cuts across any slight unevenness upon any surface which it lights – hence collar bone, neck line, arms and leg muscles are so distorted as to make the subject appear emaciated and angular. This can be avoided by slightly adjusting the beam and angle of the light without losing the dramatic effect at all, but it makes the exposure slightly longer.

There are many other forms of background, such as columns, steps and other bits of scenery, but these are only usable in a large studio and I feel do not belong here.

(b) CAMERAS AND FILMS

I have always found the most useful all-round camera to be a quarter-plate reflex with a 3·5 or 2·5 lens and speeds from one-tenth to one-thousandth. It is an economical size from every point of view, the films or plates being cheap to buy, easy to retouch, and they enlarge to 15 in by 20 in without any sign of 'grain'. After many experiments I have found that films or plates of 19° Scheiner for portraits and 32° Scheiner for action pictures are the most suitable. The very fast ones can be used for portraits but are a little lacking in gradation for such work.

147

(c) RETOUCHING, ETC.

Owing to the fact that ballet is in itself a highly specialized form of art, the photographing of dancers in action is not merely the technique of arresting movement. The photographer has to watch for and correct all possible technical faults of the dancers, of which they are usually extremely conscious. Such faults should be avoided at all costs, particularly as the camera usually exaggerates them.

'Camera angle' is of the greatest importance in making or marring a dancer. I have in mind the picture taken at a 'low angle' of a dancer considered tall for a ballerina, which exaggerated her height and distorted her figure alarmingly. Full lengths should usually be taken with the camera at waist level, but dancing photographs I take at the level of the neck line or even higher. This I have found necessary because the 'tutu' cuts the body up and gives the appearance of lengthening the legs and shortening the trunk. A similar illusion is given by the three-quarter-length *Sylphides* skirt when rotating, particularly as it is generally made with a curiously ugly short bodice. There is one danger of this method, which can, however, be avoided by 'retouching', and that is that it may give the dancer the appearance of being 'turned in' because the high angle of the

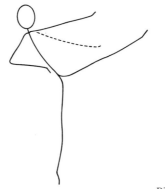

Diagram 2

camera is apt to catch the heel of the dancer in arabesque.

The arms are important to watch and should be used to full advantage in carrying out a dancer's 'line', as shown in Diagram 2, where the dancer will tend to drop her arm onto her leg, as shown by the dotted line, thus spoiling the balance of the picture. As well as being more correct, it would be better for her to do an arabesque of less height and purer quality. The foreshortening of arms, either when receding into the background or when directly pointing towards the camera, is a nightmare for the photographer and should be avoided, unless the picture brings out in some exceptional way a dancer's virtuosity or personality. Curiously enough,

in drawings such things appear correct, but in photographs they are singularly unattractive.

With regard to retouching, the most important points are as follows:

(a) Arms – elbow joints and forearm muscles.

(b) Collar bones.

(c) Bulges caused by elastic and general tight fitting of the bodice to the figure.

(d) Points – ballet shoes having square toes are extremely ugly at close quarters and these should be rounded off. Also the top ends of the tapes holding them on should always be removed.

(e) Calf muscles – highly developed in all dancers and particularly ugly.

(f) Knees – frequently lights on the knee-cap can give the appearance of protruding knees.

(g) In general all creases of the dresses and tights should be removed.

To sum up, the photographer should understand almost as much of the dancer's art as that of his own in order to achieve the cooperation which is essential, and from my experience I have found dancers extremely willing and understanding – but on no account have a mirror in the studio or there *will* be trouble!

Bibliography

GORDON ANTHONY
Markova, *Chatto and Windus*, 1935.
Ballet, *Geoffrey Bles*, 1937.
The Vic-Wells Ballet, *George Routledge*, 1938.
Leonide Massine, *George Routledge*, 1939.
Russian Ballet, *Geoffrey Bles*, 1939.
The Sleeping Princess, *George Routledge*, 1940.
Margot Fonteyn, *Gordon Anthony*, 1941.
Sadler's Wells Ballet, *Geoffrey Bles*, 1942.
Ballerina (Fonteyn), *Home and Van Thal*, 1945.
Robert Helpmann, *Home and Van Thal*, 1946.
Sadler's Wells Ballet at Covent Garden, *Home and Van Thal*, 1947.
Studies of Dancers, *Home and Van Thal*, 1948.
Margot Fonteyn, *Phoenix House*, 1950.
Alicia Markova, *Phoenix House*, 1951.

Beryl Grey, *Phoenix House*, 1952.
A Camera at the Ballet: Pioneers of the Royal Ballet, *David and Charles*, 1975.

C. W. BEAUMONT
Complete Book of Ballets, *Putnam*, 1937.

ANATOLE CHUJOY AND P. W. MANCHESTER
The Dance Encyclopedia (Revised and Expanded), *Simon and Schuster*, 1967.

The Sadler's Wells Ballet: A History and an Appreciation, *A & C Black*, 1955

MARY CLARKE
Dancers of Mercury, The Story of Ballet Rambert, *A & C Black*, 1962.

MARY CLARKE & DAVID VAUGHAN
The Encyclopedia of Dance and Ballet, *Pitman*, 1977.

ARNOLD HASKELL
Balletomania (Revised and Expanded), *Penguin*, 1980.

Ballet Annuals, *A & C Black*, 1947–61.

HORST KOEGLER
The Concise Oxford Dictionary of Ballet, *Oxford University Press*, 1977.

NINETTE DE VALOIS
Invitation to the Ballet, *The Bodley Head*, 1937.
Come Dance with Me, *Hamish Hamilton*, 1957.
Step by Step, *W H Allen*, 1977.

G. B. L. WILSON
A Dictionary of Ballet (Third edition, revised and enlarged), *A & C Black*, 1974.